Liang A-Fa

Studies in Chinese Christianity

G. Wright Doyle and Carol Lee Hamrin,
Series Editors

A project of the Global China Center

www.globalchinacenter.org

Liang A-Fa

China's First Preacher,
1789–1855

GEORGE HUNTER MCNEUR

Introduced and Edited by
Jonathan A. Seitz

PICKWICK *Publications* · Eugene, Oregon

LIANG A-FA
China's First Preacher, 1789–1855
Revised edition

Studies in Chinese Christianity

Pickwick Publications
An Imprint of Wipf and Stock Publishers
199 W. 8th Ave., Suite 3
Eugene, OR 97401

www.wipfandstock.com

ISBN 13: 978-1-49826-157-9

Cataloguing-in-Publication data:

McNeur, George Hunter.

Liang A-Fa : China's first preacher, 1789–1855 / George Hunter McNeur ; introduced and edited by Jonathan A. Seitz.

Studies in Chinese Christianity

xliv + 130 pp. ; 23 cm. Includes bibliographical references and index.

Originally published 1934.

ISBN 13: 978-1-61097-660-2

1. Liang, Afa, 1789–1855. 2. Christian biography—China. 3. Christianity—China. 4. China—Social conditions—1644–1912. I. Seitz, Jonathan. II. Title. III. Series.

BV3427 L5 M3 2013

Manufactured in the USA

Dedicated to

THREE MARGARETS

Mother—Wife—Daughter

Contents

Illustrations   *viii*

A Critical Introduction to Liang A-Fa: China's First Preacher
—Jonathan A. Seitz   *ix*

Editor's Notes on This Edition   *xxxix*

Foreword   *xli*

Preface   *xliii*

1   The Light of Sacred Story   1

2   The Making of a Prophet   7

3   Seed Time and Harvest   18

4   Brighter than the Noonday Sun   24

5   The Cost of a Bride   31

6   The Chinese Gospel   40

7   Humanized Literature   47

8   Individual Evangelism   57

9   A Double Blow   66

10   Wheat and Tares   75

11   Patriotism not Enough   81

12   God's Things and Caesar's   92

13   Go—Preach—Heal   99

14   The Last Crossing   107

15   After Many Days   115

Chinese-English Glossary   121

Index   125

Illustrations

George Hunter McNeur (1874–1953)   xi

An image of Liang from the first Chinese edition of the biography   xix

2.1   Liang A-fa's old house in Lohstun Village   14

2.2   Banyan trees on hill behind Liang A-fa's village home   15

2.3   The old watch-tower in Liang A-fa's village   15

2.4   A village school in the Liang A-fa Ancestral Temple   16

5.1   Rev. Wm. Milne, D.D.   37

5.2   From a Chinese Painting of the English Factories at Canton as they were in Dr. Morrison's Time   38

7.1   Photograph of a letter written by Liang A-fa   54

7.2   Lohtsun, the birthplace of Liang A-fa is South-West from Canton   55

9.1   Dr. Morrison with two Chinese assistants   72

9.2   From a Painting by George Chinnery of Dr. Peter Parker   73

11.1   Samchow Market   89

11.2   Liang A-fa's House on Honam, Canton   89

11.3   Liang A-fa Memorial Centre at Samchow Temporary Quarters opened 1933   90

11.4   Grave of Liang A-fa in centre of Lingnan University Campus   90

14.1   "Autumn Gold" in old age. Died some years ago in Kwangsi   113

14.2   A Christian great granddaughter of Liang A-fa with her husband and children   114

A Critical Introduction to *Liang A-Fa*

*China's First Preacher**

Jonathan A. Seitz

L iang Fa (1789–1855) is among the most compelling figures in Chinese Christian biography. He was the second known Chinese Protestant convert, and the first ordained Protestant preacher. He witnessed persecution, suffered as a confessor, outlived the major missionaries of the first generation, and appears to have been the initial theological source for the founder of the Taiping Rebellion, which was the world's largest rebellion before the twentieth century. Liang, as we will see, has been claimed in multiple histories: missions history, Chinese Protestantism, the printing press, Sino-Western exchange, the Taiping, and diplomatic history.

While foreign scholars have written Liang Fa's name in many different ways (Leang A-fa, Leang-kung-făh, and Leung Faat), we know the characters for his name because he actually wrote and published in Chinese— something that distinguishes him from every other known convert during the first decades of the London Missionary Society (LMS) mission to China and Southeast Asia (from Morrison's arrival in 1807 until his death in 1834). Details on Liang's life are distributed throughout his most famous work *Good News to Admonish the World* (1832), other short theological works, through the writings of the LMS missionaries, and in a diary he kept in 1830.

Even as many of the major missionaries (Robert Morrison, Elijah Bridgman, Karl Gützlaff, James Legge) have been the subject of recent biographies, early Chinese leaders have been bypassed. Liang is certainly ripe for such treatment, and while a new biography is justified, the model

* I, Jonathan Seitz, have composed and placed all endnotes, whether in this introduction or in McNeur's biography; none of the notes are original to McNeur.

biography from the 1930s by George Hunter McNeur (1874–1955) deserves wider availability. The Chinese version of McNeur's biography has
been regularly reprinted, but the English edition is hard to locate. My hope
is that an annotated reprint will fill this gap.

It may seem strange to be reprinting a biography that was published
almost eighty years ago. However, there are only a few sources that I have
been able to locate that were unavailable to McNeur (principally the collection of tracts, *Good News to Admonish the Ages*, which I discuss below),
and McNeur used a number of works that others have ignored. Liang is a
challenging subject for a biographer—a witness to major events, but one
who was described within the fairly narrow confines of missionary writing and his own writing. There appear to be no new newspaper articles,
memoirs, legal records, or other materials to shed light on Liang's work.
On the other hand, McNeur spent the greater part of fifty years living in the
area of Liang's birth and gathered nearly all available materials. McNeur
describes in the first chapter his own background in writing the book and
the importance of Liang's work. He had access to people who have long
since been forgotten. McNeur notes that most of Liang's family materials
were lost in a flood, and that "a few family portraits—among them one of
Liang A-fa, some worm-eaten papers, and a time-worn copy of St. Matthew's Gospel printed at Canton in 1813, are all that can found."[1] McNeur
reproduces some of this material, including a portrait, in his book, but the
current location of these materials is unknown.

In this introduction it is possible to offer some insight into Liang's
biographer, George Hunter McNeur, and into the scholarship of the last
eighty years. Thoughtful scholars have analyzed some aspects of Liang's
work, but none since McNeur have done so holistically. I also describe the
one major work of Liang's that was unavailable to McNeur, *Good News
to Admonish the Ages*, and endnote other materials that will be helpful to
those who want to learn more. I conclude by discussing several roles that
Liang modeled for Chinese Protestants. In a few years we will see the bicentennial of Liang's baptism (November 3, 2016), surely an important event
in modern Chinese Christianity.

THE HISTORY OF THE BIOGRAPHY

George Hunter McNeur (1874–1953)

McNeur's history is interesting on its own terms. Information from his granddaughter, Margaret Moore, and family histories allow us to fill in the picture more fully.[2] George Hunter McNeur (Dec. 24, 1874–1953) was born at Inchclutha in New Zealand, the second child of seven. McNeur's father was a schoolmaster and all the family were devout Presbyterians. His four younger brothers also became ministers and his sister a deaconess of that church. George filled the shoes of his older brother, James, who died at age twenty-two in 1895. He originally began a career working for a newspaper, but when James died he used the money to begin mission service. McNeur studied at Knox Theological Hall (New Zealand), then in Adelaide (Australia) and Glasgow (Scotland). He originally anticipated joining the China Inland Mission, and began some training in New Zealand, joining the Reverend Alexander Don visiting Chinese miners in the Central Otago goldfields, learning Cantonese, and earning their trust. This contact made for the decision in 1901 by the Presbyterian Church of Otago and Southland to send him as its first missionary to the villages just north of Canton, from which the miners came. Thus began the Canton Villages Mission. McNeur married Margaret (Maggie) Sinclair in 1903 in Hong Kong.

In addition to working on the Canton Villages Mission, he also taught at the American Presbyterian Seminary, which later became Canton Union Theological Seminary.

McNeur arrived in China shortly after the Boxer Rebellion, and witnessed the tumultuous years marked by the 1911 Revolution, the anti-Christian period, Chinese civil war, and World War II. McNeur wrote *Liang A-fa* during the high tide of Protestant mission in China. He appears to have known the major ecclesiastical and organizational leaders of the church. He used the language of "older" and "younger" churches that characterized this period, and it is clear that in writing *Liang A-Fa* he was writing to both Chinese and foreign Christians—certainly a challenging task.

McNeur returned to New Zealand to serve as the moderator of the Presbyterian Church in 1926–1927. In 1941 the family left China under the Japanese invasion. During his last years of his career, through to 1950, he ministered to the Chinese in Dunedin. In addition of his career work on Liang, McNeur wrote the history of New Zealand immigrant ministries to the Chinese. McNeur died in 1953, and was followed by his wife in 1957. He was the recipient of an honorary doctorate from the University of Aberdeen and is buried in Anderson's Bay Cemetery. The family biography notes that "The headstone was erected by the Chinese community in Dunedin." In addition to his biography of Liang, McNeur wrote pamphlets or books about mission work in China and among Chinese immigrants in New Zealand; he also wrote several textbooks in Chinese published in the 1950s.[3]

McNeur used a variety of materials. He drew primarily on the memoirs of the missionaries who worked most closely with Liang: Robert Morrison, William Milne, Walter Medhurst, Elijah Coleman Bridgman, David Abeel, and Samuel Wells Williams. These are the patriarchs of the early London Missionary Society mission and the American Board of Commissioners for Foreign Missions, and each relied heavily on Liang at different times and saw in him the future of the Chinese church. In particular, McNeur had access to a few crucial materials from London—a letter and journal penned by Liang which are still part of the Council for World Mission (the continuation of the London Missionary Society) collection at the School of Oriental and African Studies at London University. As far as I know, no one else has studied these Chinese materials of Liang. McNeur also reflects the missionary context in which he wrote. He mentions the *Re-Thinking Missions* report, often cites major Presbyterian preachers, refers to famous missionaries or ecumenists like Temple Gairdner and John R. Mott, and includes comments by major Chinese Christian leaders like Liu Tingfang, C. Y. Cheng, and David Z. T. Yui.

Despite considerable effort, it is still hard to tell how McNeur went about researching and writing the work. Most of the materials he used came from missionary memoirs and institutional records in English. Curiously, the Chinese version (there are only two known copies) from 1930 precedes the publication of the English version in 1934, although a translator (Hu Zanyun) is listed. This would be reprinted at least four times: in 1955, 1959, 1998, and 2001, and it was almost always one of the Chinese reprints that scholars use when citing the biography. The 1955 edition even included large reprints of parts of Liang's book *Good News to Admonish the Ages*. In the last two editions Zhu Xinran is listed as the translator. It appears that the Chinese predates the 1934 English version, the sole English edition, which can be found in perhaps a dozen libraries around the world. The versions vary slightly. The Chinese version omits many of the opening chapter quotes and features nineteen (1931) or twenty (1955) chapters, as well as one or more appendices; the 1931 Chinese edition had only one appendix (a chronology based on Alexander Wylie's work) while the 1955 edition included a longer timeline and also inserted a number of chapters from *Good News* totaling more than a hundred pages. Providing an English annotation gives us some more insight into the types of sources that McNeur relied on, as well as a bit more of his own interpretation.

McNeur is a descriptive biographer, and he brings the preacher's imagination to his work. Where there are holes in the narrative, he projects a vision of how an event might have looked or felt. Writing within and for the church, McNeur remembers a local hero and commends him to his audience. He describes many of the challenges in studying Liang, and also deals with some of the gaps in the missionary literature.

LIANG IN SECONDARY SCHOLARSHIP

There is also a helpful analytical body of writing that has sought to understand Liang's ministry. Written during the last thirty or so years, many of these works treat Liang's life, although each is limited in its focus. P. Richard Bohr has several significant works on Liang in connection to Liang's influence on the Taiping Rebellion.[4] (Taiping founder Hong Xiuquan is said to have been inspired by Liang's tracts.) Both Jonathan Spence[5] and Thomas Reilly[6] also treat this question of the relationship between Liang's works and the Taiping. There are some dangers in such a piecemeal approach.

Those studying a later generation of converts often emphasize the limits of the first generation, and writers on the Taiping sometimes read Liang too simplistically.

Two biographies of Liang exist. The earliest is McNeur's, which lists two publishing houses: a Chinese mission press and Oxford.[7] McNeur still had access to distant relatives of Liang and was able to gather a variety of materials, many no longer available.[8] A more popular biography is Bobby Sng's *I Must Sow the Seed* (1998), which is based entirely on English-language material; Sng does not appear to have had access to McNeur's biography or to Liang's Chinese-language works.[9] I believe my dissertation is the only recent thesis to treat Liang.[10] A short historical-fiction account based on McNeur's biography was published in the late 1940s.[11] Shorter articles also treat Liang's life; one of the best is Whalen Lai's article on Liang's conversion.[12] Whalen Lai has translated a fifteen-page portion of Liang's conversion account—roughly the first half—which emphasizes the discussion of sin, a recurrent theme in nonconformist missionary literature (and Reformed theology more generally).[13] Other materials on Liang can be found in the writings of early missionaries such as Walter Medhurst, David Abeel, and Elijah Bridgman, or in the writings of a later generation, including bibliographer Alexander Wylie, who published a summary of all the known early Chinese Protestant texts, including some attributed to Liang. Recently, Su Ching has written in Chinese thoughtfully about early Chinese converts, including Liang.[14] The bicentennial of Morrison's arrival in China led to some new analyses of Liang's life.[15]

GOOD NEWS: A TRACT, A MORALITY BOOK, OR SOMETHING IN BETWEEN

The major source to which McNeur lacked access is Liang's famous work, *Good News to Admonish the World*, which he never mentions by name in the biography. However, it is a document that recent scholars discuss, including Bohr, Kuhn, Lai, Reilly, and Spence. *Good News* is often labeled a tract, which is misleading unless we understand what a tract was in nineteenth-century evangelical Protestantism. *Good News* stretched to five hundred pages and included nine stand-alone chapters or *juan*.[16] Its length and eclectic composition paralleled both the English tract tradition as well as the Chinese morality-book tradition. It was a collection of writings, some republished or culled from Milne's and Medhurst's Chinese periodicals. In it, Liang says that Morrison revised some of his works.[17] Together, the nine chapters of *Good News* give us an insight into what Liang understood the teaching of Jesus to be. The name of the work is revealing. "Admonish" (*quan*) is relatively straightforward.[18] "World" (*shi*) is often also translated "ages."[19] "Good words" (*liang yan*) repeats the concern with correct speech, "good news," or, as we will see, correct conduct. Liang's surname *Liang* and the word "goodness" *liang* that appears in Liang's book are homonyms.

Bohr describes the book as an eclectic selection of excerpts from the 1823 Morrison-Milne Bible, along with ten "homilies based on evangelical themes" culled from the LMS tracts and Liang's own writings.[20] Notably, this includes the conversion account and other material. Bohr finds five main themes that influenced the Taiping, and that also act as a sketch of Liang's theology: "Monotheism and Idolatry," "Repentance and Conversion," "Moral Activism," "A New Heaven and a New Earth," and "Last Judgment."[21] These are all major themes in LMS tracts, and they also provided the material for the evangelism in which Liang engaged

Good News is primarily a collection of Bible stories, written in a Chinese style that resembles "morality books" (*shanshu*). The Morrison Collection in the Council for World Mission Collection at the School of Oriental and African Studies has at least three morality books that likewise begin with the word "admonish" or "exhort" (*quan*): "Collected exhortations and warnings" (*Quanjie leishao*), "Comprehensive book on exhorting the world" (*Quanshi quanshu*), and "Thirty poems exhorting filial piety" (*Quanxiaoshi shanshi shou*). These works tend to be written by lay Chinese religious practitioners or amateurs, rather than by scholar-officials: Liang was writing in a popular devotional style that may seem strange to contemporary Western scholars.[22] Morrison and Milne often wrote about such morality books in their English-language periodical the *Indo-Chinese Gleaner*. Cynthia Brokaw also describes this morality-book tradition, drawing in part on the library of books at London University that Morrison had collected. Brokaw writes that "morality books can be defined simply as texts that teach people to do good and avoid evil. The ledgers, like all morality books, are founded on the belief in supernatural retribution—that is, the faith that heaven or the gods will reward men who do good and punish those who do evil."[23] *Good News* thus follows a literate lay tradition that was religious in nature, commenting on individual salvation, merit attainment, and the moral life.

Philip Kuhn calls Liang's *Good News* "unsystematic, with long quotes from the Morrison-Milne translation of the Bible (in an opaquely literal classical style) interspersed with exegetical sermons by Liang in the vernacular."[24] He adds that "the character of Jehovah is strongly delineated, but that of Jesus is largely ignored," concluding that "the work's stark fundamentalist message hammers home the omnipotence of God, the degradation of sin and idolatry, and the awesome choice between salvation or damnation."[25] *Good News* is not systematic, although the statement that "Jesus is largely ignored" is hard to reconcile with an appraisal of *Good News* as primarily concerned with sin, idolatry, and salvation. In fact, redemption through Christ is a major theme.[26] *Good News* is also written in a fairly colloquial style. Reilly says that "Liang Afa's tract was very much a New Testament work," which seems natural given Liang's focus on Christ. "The Lord who saves the world" (*Jiushizhu*) is the term that Liang most often pairs with Jesus. Kuhn believes that Jesus' humanity is less important to Liang than Jesus' role as savior, which is certainly true; this is, however, a common emphasis in missionary theology, and Liang never repudiates any classical christological formulation. As has often been true in Christian history, Christ's divinity is emphasized while his humanity is assumed or ignored.

Reilly seems to offer a related criticism of Liang's theology. He faults Liang for a limited worldview where a focus on salvation trumps social ethics, and a sacred/secular division prevails: "Liang went out of his way to exclude any discussion of economic, political, or social consequences for the religious ideas he explained, in effect polarizing the world of religion and the world of government and society."[27] Reilly says that Liang did this by choosing only Bible passages that reinforced his views, "passages that emphasized Protestant themes of individual, as opposed to national or social, salvation." Moreover, Liang, via the LMS missionaries, borrowed "the idiosyncratic Catholic Basset" gospel harmony, adapting it to major LMS themes.[28] Reilly also finds that Liang "included little from the Old Testament and no passages from the historical books; he referred only briefly to the experience of Israel delivered from Egypt; he did not list the Ten Commandments, though he did refer to Moses and did mention some of the individual commandments (given the prominent role of the Decalogue in the Taiping movement, this is a significant omission); he referred to the Jews, but he did not discuss their special role as 'God's chosen people'; and he dedicated only a few verses to the history of the kingdom of Israel."[29] He says that "In short, he provided an abundance of allusions to an otherworldly, individual salvation, but only meager mention of this-worldly, historical, national salvation (indeed, his arrangement of the biblical selections violates the historical arrangement in the Bible itself)."[30] The criticism is true enough, but it asks too much of the first generation preacher and printer to also write a formal theology and advocate for national salvation. Liang's tract is indeed about "saving the world," so it is natural that soteriology, the doctrine of salvation, and Jesus' role as savior become the main themes. Liang's approach is actually quite broad. He has a description of creation at the outset, proceeds to a range of other topics, and includes some discussion of the end of time. (McNeur defends Liang's writing style and approach in chapter 10.)

Clearly, Liang's writing had a very particular audience in mind, mostly literate Chinese in southeast China and parts of Southeast Asia. For this reason, scholars probably expect too much from him when they raise these types of issues, and they often forget the context in which he worked.[31] The Ten Commandments were a major theme in the broader LMS curriculum that students in fact were required to memorize as they memorized the catechisms. They were probably distributed in tract or catechism form along with *Good News*, so it is natural that they were not included in *Good News*. The Chinese Bible in its entirety had been in print for a decade, and the New Testament for two decades, when Liang wrote his work. Missionaries even circulated a stand-alone version of Exodus, apart from that included in their Bibles.[32] Since Liang apparently distributed individual chapters separately, he likely understood his admittedly idiosyncratic selections as serving a variety of purposes: some would focus on creation, others on idolatry, while another provided his own witness, and so forth.[33]

I find that Liang did have an ethical thrust that included at least some nominal idea of national salvation. Liang's scope was universal, reflected in his emphasis on "saving the world," of which China was a crucial piece. (This is addressed below in the section on Liang as social critic.) While Liang does not frequently mention China, he does use the word several times. Moreover, Liang's diverse roles allowed him to articulate a particular understanding of the Christian life, which he hoped would lead to the transformation of his people. It is certainly true that Liang's writing is archetypically Protestant, prioritizing Scripture and salvation through Christ, and a piety that emphasizes hard work and an otherworldly focus. Liang's social commitments conform to the ascetic religion that Max Weber described, as well as to the archetypal evangelical conversions described by William James in *The Varieties of Religious Experience*.[34] The early missionaries tended to come from pious families who worked at crafts or on farms, and they emphasized a type of religious devotion that combined thrift and hard work. They stressed a life of labor and proclamation, and also were part of broader, trans-Atlantic evangelical movements that called for holiness and the reform of the nation.

Good News also has two unique sections that are not Scripture translations: the conversion account (chapter 6 of *Good News*) and the polemical section against Chinese religion (chapter 1). Neither Kuhn nor Reilly notes these accounts. Wylie's summary notes the polemical essay—"an exposure of the idolatry of China"—but ignores the conversion account. Wylie gives a general summary of each chapter, listing the relevant scripture passages.[35] Wylie also notes that portions of *Good News* are repackaged as two other booklets, *Selection of Important Words to Admonish the Age* and *Important Discourse on Seeking Happiness and Escaping Misery*.[36] These in turn were built on earlier LMS publications, including the *Chinese Monthly* and various tracts. This underscores the problem of treating Liang's work as a flawed systematic theology rather than as a unique contribution to the broader corpus of hybrid LMS Chinese works.

Scholarship since McNeur has aided in developing the broader context of Liang's work, and has also helped with particular concerns (the introduction of new printing technologies, the translation of the Bible, and so on). Lai's article on Liang's baptism and the work of scholars like Kuhn and Reilly on the Taiping are also major contributions. Nonetheless, McNeur's early study of Liang's contribution to the development of Christianity in China seems especially significant. Several themes in particular seem important.

LIANG'S ENDURING LEGACY

Now that we have surveyed the scholarship on Liang from McNeur to the present, it may be helpful to review several recurring themes in Liang's life. Scholars tend to treat Liang's tract as background for their own interests (Protestant theology, missions institutions, the Taiping, etc.), and often give the impression that they have not consulted the work thoroughly. Liang remains the sole source of early Chinese Protestant writing, and his work demands a more critical study, something that I can only begin here. Liang assumed a number of key roles: convert, firstfruits, confessor, ordained leader, evangelist, polemicist, social critic, and theologian. Each of these roles deepened or shaded his understanding of what it meant to be a Christian. Scholars have neglected several unique aspects in Liang's writing, including a polemic against Chinese religion and Liang's naming of God.

In most cases McNeur develops these themes, but the information in *Good News* and elsewhere helps to expand them. In these cases, we have Liang's unmediated words to explain what it meant to follow Christ. Many of these are topics that McNeur himself develops. Virtually none of the later scholars appear to have read McNeur, and my sense is that they often miss Liang's significance in the early years of Chinese Protestant Christianity. As the convert par excellence and the major church leader of his generation, he provides a fascinating study.

An image of Liang from the first Chinese edition of the biography.

Liang as Convert

A notable feature of Liang's book is that it includes his own conversion account. Milne's baptism of Liang is particularly revealing because there are several versions: two in English and one in Chinese. In Milne's own rendering, the emphasis is on typical missionary concerns: the integrity of the conversion, acceptance of doctrinal statements, and fears of material incentives for conversion. Liang's telling is largely unconcerned with these problems, focusing on what it means to follow Christ and to do goodness. McNeur draws principally on the narratives offered in Morrison and Medhurst. Liang's narrative may be questioned on the basis that it was published sixteen years after the fact, but Whalen Lai finds the account to be rooted in a "core experience of which we need not doubt."[37] Liang's focus is evangelistic, and rather than focusing on Milne's questions, he tends to remember the event for its meaning in his life and for the transformation it marked.

I treat Liang's conversion in depth elsewhere, but several of the most compelling aspects of it are worth noting here.[38] Where the missionaries inevitably emphasized the ways in which the conversion matched church requirements and showed a sincerity of faith, Liang highlights the ways in which he understood faith in Christ. He refers to an earlier period where he followed other gods, but ultimately he rejected these in favor of the "merits of Christ." He describes his path from working in the mission carving blocks to knowing Morrison and Milne and then finally to baptism. He expresses enthusiasm at being baptized, and at the ceremony asks if he will receive a special sign or name. Instead, he is told that the sign of a Christian is doing good *xingshan*. He takes as a penname "the one who studies goodness" (*Xueshanzhe*). Liang sees his baptism as a recognition by the missionary of his deep faith. He lives out his life with integrity and becomes the archetype for future converts.

Liang's Family as Firstfruits

As we shall see, Liang's conversion went hand in hand with that of his family. Liang inched the church onwards, baptizing his wife and establishing a Christian family. McNeur reconstructs the event, saying that there would have been Scripture reading, "earnest prayer," and perhaps a "hymn of praise may have been chanted."[39] He concludes that "as this ignorant young Chinese woman, the babe strapped on her back, took the vow to turn from idols to Christ, and her workman husband sprinkled the water of the holy sacrament upon her bowed head, no magnificent cathedral could have been more really the house of God."[40] This is the totality of what we know about the baptism of Liang's wife. I find no detailed description of it in the writing of the missionaries. Apparently, she never went to the mission in Malacca or left the Canton region, and neither Morrison nor Milne record meeting her. Surprisingly, we have no recorded discussions among the missionaries of how to handle such a baptism. (Liang's baptism of his own wife must have transgressed the ecclesiastical rules of the missionaries, who would have expected an ordained minister to preside over the sacrament of baptism.) Similarly, there is no celebration of the first female convert, as we might expect. McNeur gives us a name for Liang's wife—her surname was Lai. He notes that Liang returned to Milne in Malacca in 1821 and that for Liang's wife, "unable to read, knowing only the barest rudiments of Christian truth, alone in the heathen community in which she had been brought up, hers was the harder part."[41] Women are often invisible figures in the missionary writings, and we have little sense of what female domestics or others worked with the missionaries—this brief description of Liang's wife is part of the sparse information available to us.

Morrison first mentioned Liang's wife in a letter recorded in his memoirs on November 10, 1823: "His aged father rejects the truth, but his wife, he says, has become a Christian, and he has promised to bring his infant son for baptism."[42] In a postscript he adds that "Afa, whom our dear Milne baptized, has led his wife to embrace Christianity, and proposes to bring his little son to me to be baptized."[43] It may be that after baptizing his wife, Liang had been encouraged to have his son baptized by an ordained pastor (and thus one of the missionaries). Ten days later, on November 20, Morrison wrote that Liang, "our Chinese fellow-disciple, brought his son Leang-tsin-tĭh [*Liang Jinde*], 'entering on virtue,' and had him baptized in the name of God, the Father, Son, and Spirit." Morrison then exclaimed "Oh that this small Christian family may be the means of spreading the truth around them in this pagan land."[44] These baptismal accounts leave as much unclear as is explained. Reformed understandings of baptism would have been stretched in a situation in which there was no formal "church," and "worship" consisted of one or two missionaries, a convert or two, and other workers in the mission who were encouraged to attend.[45]

Nonetheless, for new Christians, family could also be a source of conflict. In 1820, the *Indo-Chinese Gleaner* records an article about someone who is probably Liang (the only possible alternative, Tsae, had died in 1818), when Amicus (the missionary penname that likely referred to Robert Morrison) writes:

> Not long ago, a Christian son, a poor man in China, addressed his pagan father to persuade him to receive Christianity. The old man said: 'How can you be so conceited as to imagine that your novel opinion is right, and that I your father, and my fathers for forty centuries, and all the rich men, and learned men, and powerful Mandarins, and even the Emperor himself are wrong—it cannot be. I will conform to the religion of my country, and my fathers, and follow the great men of the land in their opinions and practices.[46]

We do not ultimately know what happened to the father of the "poor man in China." In an 1827 letter to "the directors" Liang wrote: "I thank the Lord for his wondrous mercy, in converting my whole family."[47] McNeur notes the tortuous path that Liang's family would take, but eventually locates a granddaughter's return to Christianity, which the missionary biographer read as the fruits of Liang's ministry.

Liang as Confessor

Liang notes that after he revised and printed two hundred copies of a "small book," *Outline Concerning the Salvation of the World,* he was "falsely accused" and imprisoned.[48] There was a hearing or trial. Liang said that he was not allowed to speak, and was scolded for making [printing] a book of Jesus and believing in his truth. Immediately after the trial, said Liang, he was jailed. While there, he quietly thought about, or meditated upon, the way (*mo xiang dao*). He thought on how the book described Jesus saving the world. All of this was to "admonish people to depart from evil to follow the goodness of the good book."[49]

After a couple of days, Liang reports that Morrison heard of his suffering and sent people to talk to the official. Before he was released, his legs were beaten thirty times with a large stick "until they flowed with blood."[50] Liang's beating seems to have fallen somewhere in the midrange of Qing punishment; certainly, it indicated more than a minor crime. Nancy Park writes that "officials who were convicted of private offenses would be subject to criminal penalties ranging from ten blows of the light bamboo to 100 blows of the heavy bamboo."[51] Liang also reported being blackmailed for seventy dollars. Afterwards, Liang thanked the great grace of the Lord who redeems and saves the world. Liang says that after this he was even more careful not to sin or offend.[52] Here and elsewhere, Liang seems to imply that calamity is the result of sin (in another situation, Liang blames a drought on such sin).

A recurring theme in the early literature about Liang is his role as "confessor," which in the classical Christian tradition meant one who suffered for the faith. (I do not believe there were any who were martyred in the first generation, although others, like Liang, suffered for their faith.) When Liang is reintroduced in the second volume of Morrison's memoirs, Morrison writes that Liang "has been called to suffer for righteousness' sake" and that Liang has "truly felt the power of his divine truth, and is an example of the utility of the Bible in this idolatrous country."[53] Indeed, Morrison's memoirs mention persecution or suffering in connection with Liang at least a half-dozen times.[54]

Su Ching provides a short summary of this episode, drawn from Morrison's account to the LMS directors:

> Two weeks before finishing the translation [of an edition of the whole Bible], Liang Afa, a printer who had been baptized by Milne at Malacca and had recently returned to Canton was captured. Shortly before the incident, Morrison gave him seventy dollars to cut the blocks of a small work by himself . . . *Chiu-shih-lu ch'uo* [sic]-*yao lüeh-chieh*, Miscellaneous Exhortations, and to cast off 200 copies. The books and blocks were taken altogether and burnt. Before he was beaten, Liang defended himself by saying that his book was not bad but exhorted people to be virtuous. The magistrate replied, 'Your book is stuff and nonsense. I punish you for going beyond seas!'[55]

Wylie also provides an extensive description of the book, which is not available in the IDC collection and does not appear to be extant.[56]

With the White Lotus Rebellions still in recent memory, and ongoing fears of revolution, Liang's preaching represented a possible threat. For Liang, the punishment tested his faith, clearly arguing against a shallow conversion. It marked him as a leader willing to suffer for his faith.

Liang as Ordained Leader

The possible ordination of a local evangelist was early raised for the LMS mission, especially since there were few missionaries, and their health was always unreliable. In a letter dated November 3, 1820, Milne is said to have asked: "Should A-fa continue steadfast in his profession, and in the pursuit of knowledge, and in his desire for usefulness for a year or two longer, would it be advisable to ordain him before his return to China [from Malacca], that he might be qualified to administer Christian ordinances in case of your death, or in case of any convert being obtained who could not come to you for baptism?"[57] Presbyterian or Reformed theology often relates ordination to three marks of the church (1) proclamation or preaching, (2) administration of the two sacraments of baptism and the Lord's Supper, and (3) church discipline. This meant that a potential missionary absence raised serious problems. When, subsequently, Milne died and Morrison returned to England in December 1823 for an extended sabbatical, Liang's ordination became necessary for the integrity of the mission. In Morrison's memoirs, the editor wrote that Morrison "had strongly urged upon the Christian community in Europe and America, the necessity of having a successor," but that this did not happen. Therefore, "to insure the continuation of Christian ordinances among the few who had renounced idolatry . . . he dedicated Leang-Afã, who had for eight years given evidence of his qualifications for the work, to the office of Evangelist among his countrymen."[58]

Liang, in his own account, describes a more personal rationale for his ordination, focusing on how it reflected on his faithfulness, dependency, and integrity. In *Good News*, he writes that since "Old Mr. Morrison had seen that my wife and son all faithfully worshipped and believed in the way of the Lord. He considered me a sincere person, who studied the scriptures and wanted to study and understand the true way of righteousness, in order to have the knowledge of a pastor; later on he laid hands on me [*anshou*], and ordered me to admonish the people of every place, and from then until now, for many years and months, I have joyfully served."[59] This also suggests that in naming his book *Good News to Admonish the World*, Liang may have been echoing "Great Commission" language at the end of Matthew, equating "admonishing the world" with "admonishing the people of all places." The word I have translated here as "laid on hands" is the contemporary word for "ordination." Liang clearly understood this laying on of hands as investing great power; distinguishing no differences (evangelist, pastor, missionary, and so forth), Liang uses the word "shepherd," which eventually becomes one of the two main Chinese words for *pastor*. At the same time, it is significant that the missionaries apparently were called by the honorific "mister" or "teacher," as in Liang's writing, or "teacher" (*laoshi*), a term of respect.

For Liang, the account of ordination flows naturally from that of conversion, explaining his Christian vocation and work as evangelist. He does not include the probable missionary rationale, that ordination is necessary for the correct administration of sacraments. Functionally, little appears to change, except that subsequently Liang is apparently formally sanctioned to baptize and preach and was added to the LMS payroll. Significantly, in his description of his ordination, Liang reads the ritual as recognition of his sincerity, his study, and the conversion of his family.

The question of what ordination "as an evangelist" meant for Liang remains unclear. Morrison's memoirs refer to Liang as an evangelist.[60] Mc-Neur treats the question in greater depth below but writes helpfully, "It is quite evident from the subsequent statements by missionaries associated with the evangelist that Dr. Morrison's action was accepted as involving full ordination to the Christian ministry."[61] Liang's ordination as evangelist was significant on a number of levels. No comparable ordination occurred in the first generation, and Liang remained an important figure until his death.

Liang as Evangelist

By the time of Morrison's return from furlough, Liang had prepared a small volume that Morrison described as a commentary on Hebrews and a small essay called "The True Principles of the World's Salvation."[62] Liang's role in the early 1820s seems to have been a combination of printer, student, teacher, and evangelist. McNeur treats this in detail. Like most of the workers, Liang found in Christianity a job that combined tradesman and intellectual, printer and preacher.

Morrison relates some interesting stories of Liang's interactions with other Chinese. At one point, Morrison tells a story (supposedly recorded by Liang himself in some form, perhaps in the diary) about Liang's conversation with a fellow passenger on a boat. After Liang introduced the subject of Christianity and Scripture, the other passenger quoted Mencius to him: "It would be better for mankind to have no books, than to believe everything contained in books."[63] Liang responds with a statement of faith, which in Medhurst's account, cited another statement of Mencius: "A good man may be deceived by a distorted representation of facts, but cannot be deluded so as to believe things absolutely absurd."[64] The account and others like it indicate that Liang was the leading evangelist in the LMS mission, and one of the most creative voices for the indigenization of Christianity in China. Liang evangelized in a variety of contexts: schools and hospitals, exam centers, as well as among fellow villagers, friends and family. McNeur's work below shows how Liang was frequently more adept than the missionaries, who were limited by language, time, or Qing law.

Liang the Polemicist

Christian polemic was often a response to local polemical works (for instance, elite critiques of Buddhism and local religious belief) but may also be seen as particularly Protestant with a focus on superstition and idolatry. Not surprisingly, these critiques, which were developed in conversation with LMS helpers and other Chinese acquaintances, show up in Liang's work. A frequent theme was rejection of idols, of "spirits, buddhas, and bodhisattvas." Liang's work in chapter one of *Good News* is more integrated—combined into an entire section—and more thorough, showing his closer knowledge of common religious practice and local folk beliefs than the missionaries.

The polemical section starts within ten pages of the introduction in *Good News*. It is titled "People of the World's Superstitions and Varieties of Gods, Buddhas, and Bodhisattvas," and covers more than twenty pages.[65] The title's focus on "superstition" repeats a major interest of the missionaries. This section is also one of those reprinted as a separate tract.[66] Liang begins by affirming that it was the Great Lord of Heaven and Earth who made heaven and earth and the myriad things. Repeating the missionary catechisms, Liang says that the people's nature was originally good and without evil. Liang recounts how the good nature became disordered (*luan*) and the people gradually departed from goodness. They had an evil root (*egen*) in their hearts and they followed evil. The snake demon (*shemo*) often came up to the world and introduced a pernicious seduction in the hearts of people. For this reason, said Liang, in every generation those who follow evil become more numerous, and those who love to walk in the ways of good become fewer. For Liang, good and bad are the major categories of human ontology. Liang explained that each did what he or she wanted, and evil increased.

Gradually, this comes to a discussion of idolatry. Although the Great Lord of Heaven is the true creator, people do no not know how to worship him/it. Liang says that "instead, people worship the idols that they make with their own hands as gods. Therefore, until this day the four classes of people (scholars, farmers, workers, and merchants), those of higher and lower levels, use their own ideas to produce the images of idols, gods, and buddhas to worship, using paper or writing characters, producing images of stone or wood boards or carved words, mud, four sided stone, three-point stone, fired tile, and all types of materials."[67] They fashioned two images of Wenchang and Kuixing [names for the God of Literature], as a god.[68] Liang notes that many people worship these gods hoping for scholarly advancement, even if they never succeed. The section includes a discussion of the "three religions" or "three teachings" (*sanjiao*), which Liang characterizes as Ruism ("Confucianism"), Sakyamunism (Buddhism), and Daoism, using the classical formulation of *ru shi dao*.

The focus on idolatry is sometimes roughly worded. Liang speaks of "monks who concentrate on deceiving men and women to worship Buddhas, Buddhas of the Western Heavens or the Pure Land [*jileshijie* The Sukhavati World]."[69] Liang complains that "the monks do no good things" and that they "beg for food in the street." This type of negative evaluation continues.

Liang's polemic is interesting because it includes several related criticisms. Some are theological, where idolatry is the major problem, paired with superstition. For Liang, God as Creator is contrasted with the idolatrous constructions of humans. Just as Liang's baptism involved no sign but doing good, so Christian faithfulness is fundamentally opposed to idols that block the path to God. Liang more specifically rejects categories of idols, listing gods by name; categories of practice, such as witchcraft; as well as the more general problems of "superstition." Liang's polemic also included social criticism. Like the LMS missionaries, Liang rejected monastic celibacy and the use of any images, emphasizing the significance of worshiping a creating God. Such a worldview conveyed a certain type of social piety.

Conversion means turning to something, and it typically entails a major reformulation of prior belief or practice. Conversion may be coded as intensification or transformation, but in the case of conversion to a world religion, a negative aspect often occurs. For Liang, the polemic against Chinese religion is explained in several ways. In his prior practice, merit accumulation or Guanyin worship failed to solve the problem of sin or human demerit. Eventually, on the path to baptism, Liang came to accept a Reformed understanding of salvation that involved a rejection of Chinese religious systems of salvation, emptying the pantheon of deities and replacing it with a christological doctrine of salvation. Liang's new understanding accepted the missionary criticism of Chinese religion as superstition or idolatry. While he phrased it in a way that offends some modern sensibilities, Liang understood the polemic as a significant aspect of his conversion.

Liang as Theologian

Andrew Walls has said that while the first generation of missionaries distinguished themselves as linguists, historians, religionists, and students of local culture, they rarely produced creative theology. Their primary emphasis was on translation of the Scriptures and doctrinal instruction. Liang A-Fa also follows this model. He probably did not see himself creating anything new or as teaching anything that went beyond the basic instruction of the Bible, but he showed great creativity in several areas.

The most original aspect of Liang's writing may be his naming of God.[70] Given the three most common choices of "god" (*shen*), "heaven" (*tian*), and "ruler on high" (*shangdi*), Liang elected to combine all three into the title *Shentian Shangdi*. This becomes his normative name for God, such that phrases like "son of God" are translated as "son of the Heavenly God on High" (*Shentian Shangdi zhi Zi*). In this sense, Liang circumvented the bitter debates that preoccupied missionaries in the next generations.

Liang's names for the Trinity otherwise resemble those used by Morrison. Liang often describes Jesus as "Jesus, Savior of the World" (*Jiushizhu Yesu*). Just as God's name is a four-character comprehensive term, Liang normally describes Jesus with the prefix "Savior." The Holy Spirit remains as "Godly Wind" (*Shenfeng, Shengfeng* or *Shengshenfeng*). (This name would later be replaced with "Holy/Divine Spirit/Soul" [*Shengling*].)[71]

Another interesting choice is Liang's name for the Hebrew word for God, YHWH or *Yahweh*, which is a more appropriate choice than Morrison's initial transliteration. Liang uses a combination of characters that could be literally translated as something like "Fiery Father God of China" (*Shen Yehuohua*), but that also approximates the pronunciation of YHWH. Liang's description of God the Father thus is a four-character name like the name of God—and the names of many Chinese deities. The term combines meaning and pronunciation, and could perhaps be translated simply as "God Yehuohua," or "Yahweh God." The four characters stand in for the unpronounceable Hebrew name for God, and the title combines a generic word for God with the characters for "grandfather," "fire," and "China." It is an evocative name, presenting the vision of an aged patriarch, the God who moved through the exodus as fire, and cares for China.

At times, Reilly suggests that the strangeness of Jesus' name in China was a barrier to full indigenization.[72] This is a surprising objection, since the name "Jesus" and the title "Christ" have usually been transliterated or transcribed in Christian history (as in English). The transliteration of names for Jesus and YHWH was balanced by the combination with a Chinese title (savior *jiushizhu* for Jesus and God *shen* for YHWH). Transliteration was also a familiar tradition in China, and was common in the use of Buddhist names. Despite Reilly's objection, the titles Liang used for Jesus also echo early translations in the Christian tradition.[73] The four-character formulation, use of a title, and combination of characters in a phonetic pattern was thus not entirely alien. Christian movements have historically advocated the translation of general terms for God and accepted the translatability of even such important terms as "lord" or "savior." Chinese Christians quickly followed suit.[74] At the same time, they tended to transliterate proper names and sometimes titles.

Each of Liang's terms for the persons of the Trinity reflected a combination of indigenous and foreign traditions. Appropriation, amalgamation, and reconfiguration allowed for new possibilities. In many cases, these terms were taken from earlier Catholic-Chinese encounters, and adapted or changed in light of local opinion.

Liang as Critic of Chinese Society

First-generation Christianity is sometimes criticized for its focus on otherworldly salvation. This may be broadly true—Liang's main focus was evangelistic—but even in the first quarter century of Chinese Protestantism, there was already a coherent critique of Chinese society. Liang's social criticism repeated that of the LMS missionaries. Just as the missionaries rejected English vice (alcohol, the slave trade, the opium trade, non-Christian literature, and the like), Liang readily adapted an understanding of Christian purity that called into question some Chinese practices. I originally thought of Liang's ethic as a type of evangelical nationalism, where the nation is seen as spiritually redeemable. Now I tend to see Liang's salvific vision as encompassing a world conversion that includes nations and peoples and is thus adaptable to China and Chinese people. Liang does not himself take this in the direction of millennialism or a theology of Christ's return for the purpose of saving China, but Liang's successors (especially the Taiping) clearly do. Liang occasionally mentions China *Zhongguo* by name in *Good News*, usually with reference to Chinese religion or the Chinese people, or simply as an aside.[75] He does not create a fully formed "Chinese Christianity," but takes the first steps in this direction.

We already saw that one of the two major creative projects of Liang's was a criticism of Chinese religion. While Liang apparently stayed clear of any direct condemnation of the Qing government, he adopted the shared missionary and Chinese rejection of opium use and the opium trade. Alexander Wylie credits Liang, together with Ira Tracy, in writing at least two tracts: *Incentives to Abandon Opium* (1835) and *Address of the Singapore Agricultural and Horticultural Society to the Chinese Agriculturists* (1837).[76] According to Jonathan Spence, in *Good News*, when Liang writes about the story of the rich young man who asks what is necessary to enter the Kingdom of Heaven, he not only repeats Jesus' answer, but also "adds one prohibition of his own: not to smoke opium, a vice as bad as any of the others."[77] I do not find mention of opium in the section of *Good News* cited in Spence, but Spence may have read a different tract or examined a different section. Missionaries, both Protestant and Catholic, often targeted opium in their social critiques. It may be, as Dikötter, Laamann, and Zhou assert that "the image of 300 million souls hopelessly enslaved by the 'pernicious drug' represented a powerful tool in legitimizing missionary activities."[78] At the same time, it clearly fed into a broader criticism of vice that characterized the missions of that era. It is important to note that this criticism was sometimes undermined by missionary cooperation with the British government. For instance, Liang's early mentor Morrison worked for the East India Company, which was heavily involved in the opium trade. John Robert Morrison, Robert Morrison's son, helped negotiate the 1842 Nanjing Treaty that ended the Opium Wars, and Liang's son, A-teh, went to work for the Chinese Maritime Customs led by the British. Liang's cowritten tracts highlight the fact that from the beginning Protestants were concerned about the opium trade, even though their actions sometimes inadvertently encouraged it.

Liang was part of this broader effort to create a Christian lifestyle in China. Diana Carroll finds that "the missionaries' compassion and empathy sprang from the same roots as the humanitarian and reforming zeal which drove and inspired many of their compatriots to campaign in Britain against slavery, child labour, foul conditions in prisons, slum housing and similar social evils of their time."[79] Moreover, both missionaries and converts came from working-class backgrounds and emphasized a life of piety, thrift, and work. Liang seems to have attached himself to an evangelical social piety that was cautiously respectful of the state, opposed to a wide assortment of vice, Sabbatarian and disciplined in its practice, and focused on Biblical transmission. In his 1830 travel journal, he assiduously noted every seventh day, marking it off as the Sabbath. The record also suggests that Liang attached this piety to specific Chinese teachings, including filial piety, iconoclasm, and the scholarly life.

Although several scholars seem to imply that Liang lacked a social ethic, Jessie Lutz finds that "Liang and Li Zhenggao, along with Hong Xiuquan, were searching for a doctrine to save China and believed that they had found it in Christianity."[80] Lutz mentions Liang's emphasis against "drunkenness, debauchery, violence, lying, and lack of filial duty," as well as an emphasis on the Ten Commandments and the Holy Spirit which "was the means to redemption of both the individual and Chinese society." It certainly seems accurate to say that Liang had a social-salvific vision that encompassed all humans and included a specific place for China or Chinese people. He did not seek political transformation, but he proposed a faith with strong political, social, and ethical dimensions.

CONCLUSION

In the following pages, McNeur provides a more straightforward narrative of Liang's life than these major points I have identified. Nonetheless, I hope this introduction gives some sense of the way in which Liang was significant in early Chinese Protestantism, and how he has been interpreted in the intervening years. Liang's own words in Chinese add something to the account given by the missionaries and recorded in McNeur's biography. They also show how Liang understood his own conversion, his calling as a leader, his suffering, and his writing. Secondary scholarship has occasionally offered deep insight, but more often attention to Liang has been only glancing, refracted through focus on a related subject. Liang still warrants deeper study, and I hope that this annotated reprint of McNeur's biography of the first great Chinese Protestant saint will encourage such study.

McNeur, writing at the midpoint between Liang's life and our own, saw the ways in which Liang had become a model of Christian faith. In some respects, Chinese Protestantism today seems to be building toward a new golden age, perhaps similar to the era McNeur saw in the 1930s when he wrote the biography. Christians in China certainly number in the tens of millions, and the disapora church is equally vibrant. Nonetheless, Christianity is still a minority religion, and many followers are first-generation converts. McNeur's study is still helpful today, and tells an important chapter in Chinese Protestantism. Although it has been regularly reprinted in Chinese, it has been largely unavailable to English speakers. McNeur also helps us to remember that Liang's story is significant in its own right, and not just as missionary biography. McNeur's telling is a helpful reconstruction of the life of one of modern Christianity's major figures.

Notes

1. See p. 3 below.

2. Personal correspondence with Margaret Moore, granddaughter of George H. Mc-Neur, September 23, 2009. Moore shared several documents with me, including a talk and letters by her mother Jean Moore, McNeur's daughter, a short biography, and some academic materials including a bibliography.

3. The McNeur family archives are part of the Hocken Library at Otago: *G. H. McNeur and McNeur Family Papers*, 1813–1992 (ARC 038). McNeur's works include George Hunter McNeur, *The Chinese in Our Midst* (Christchurch, NZ: Presbyterian Women's Missionary Union, 1951); George Hunter McNeur, *Viewing and Visiting the Canton Villages* (Dunedin, NZ: Foreign Missions Committee, 1907); George Hunter McNeur, *The Church and the Chinese in New Zealand* (Christchurch and Dunedin: Presbyterian Bookroom, 1951). McNeur published several books or pamphlets early in his ministry, including *Feeling the Way in the Canton Villages* (n.p.: Foreign Missions Committee, 1902); *Canton Villages Mission: First Letters of Rev. George H. McNeur* (Dunedin, NZ: Otago Daily Times and Witness) and *"The Fairer Britain of the Southern Seas": New Zealand, her Chinese and other immigrants; an essay read before the Canton Missionary Conference, March 25th* 1903 (Canton, China: China Baptist Publication Society, 1903). He also published some works to assist missionaries in their training: George Hunter McNeur, *The Missionary in Changing China* (Dunedin NZ: Otago Daily Times & Witness Papers, 1935); *The Missionary Beginning Cantonese* (n.p.: 1911). The books he published in Chinese, under his Chinese name Mai Zhenen, were studies of ministry, prayer, and mission: Mai Zhenen, *Mu Fan Xue* (Xianggang: Xianggang Shengshu Gonghui, 1953); Mai Zhenen, *Qi Dao de Dao Shi* (Xianggang: Xianggang Shengshu Gonghui, 1953); Mai Zhenen, *Xuan Dao Xue* (Xianggang: Shengshu Gonghui, 1953). Mai Zhenen, *Qi Dao de Dao Shi* (Xianggang: Xianggang Shengshu Gonghui, 1953). Worldcat lists English versions of two of these books published in Shanghai, presumably in English: *Homiletics* (1939) and *Handbook on Pastoral Theology* (1938).

4. P. Richard Bohr, "Liang Fa's Quest for Moral Power," 35–46, in Barnett and Fairbank, eds., *Christianity in China: Early Protestant Missionary Writings*; P. Richard Bohr, "Jesus, Christianity and Rebellion in China: The Evangelical Roots of the Taiping Heavenly Kingdom," 613–62, in Roman Malek, ed., *The Chinese Face of Jesus Christ*, vol. 2 (Sankt Augustin: Institut Monumenta Serica, 2002); P. Richard Bohr, "The Theologian as Revolutionary: Hung Hsiu-ch'üan's Religious Vision of the Taiping Heavenly Kingdom," 912–21, in Yen-p'ing Hao and Hsiu-mei Wei, eds., *Tradition and Metamorphosis in Modern Chinese History: Essays in Honor of Professor Kwang-Ching Liu's Seventy-Fifth Birthday*, vol. 2 (Taipei: ZhongyangYanjiu Yuan, 1998).

5. Jonathan D. Spence, *God's Chinese Son: The Taiping Heavenly Kingdom of Hong Xiuquan* (New York: Norton, 1997).

6. Thomas H. Reilly, *The Taiping Heavenly Kingdom: Rebellion and the Blasphemy of Empire* (Seattle: University of Washington Press, 2004).

7. George Hunter McNeur, *China's First Preacher, Liang Afa* (Shanghai: Kwang Hsueh Publishing House; Oxford University Press, China Agency, 1934). The earlier Chinese version is George Hunter McNeur, *Zhonghua zui zao de budaozhe Liang Fa,* trans. Hu Canyun (Shanghai: Guangxue Hui Chu Ban, 1931).

8. Ibid., 4.

9. Bobby Sng, *I Must Sow the Seed: Liang Afa: China's First Preacher* (Singapore: Trinity Theological College, 1998).

10. Jonathan A. Seitz, "The Comparative 'Merits" of Conversion: Early Chinese Protestantism (1803–1840) in Formation" (PhD diss., Princeton Theological Seminary, 2007).

11. Joyce Reason, *Bold Smuggler (Liang a-Fa, 1789–1855)* (London: Eagle, 1948).

12. Whalen Lai, "The First Chinese Christian Gospel: Liang A-Fa's 'Good Words to Admonish the World,'" *Ching Feng* 38/2 (May 1995) 83–105.

13. Ibid., 84–90, excerpted portions from *Quan shi liang yan,* VI, 5b–10b, 290–300, in one continuous quotation. He does not include the account that occurs on pages 300–310, which he intended for another article.

14. Su Ching, *Zhongguo Kai Men! [China: Open!]* (Hong Kong: Jidujiao Zhongguo Zongjiao Wenhua Yanjiushe, 2005).

15. Duan Qi, *Cong Liang Fa kan Jidujiao zai Zhongguo zaoqi de chuangjiao fangfa [From Liang Fa Looking at Early Chinese Missionary Methods],* 683–700, in Lin Jinqiang, Wu Ziming, and Xing Fuzeng, eds., *Zi xi cu dong: Jidujiao lai Hua er bai nian lunji [East Meets West: Essays Celebrating the Bicentennial of Protestant Christianity in China]* (Hong Kong: Jidujiao Wenyi Chubanshe, 2009).

16. Liang Fa, *Quan shi liang yan [Good News to Admonish the Ages].* Taibei Shi: Taiwan xue sheng shu ju, 1965. This is the standard reprint, made from a copy in the New York Public Library, with a preface and introduction. Hereafter *Good News.*

17. Ibid., 305.

18. Interestingly, at one point a major early Chinese-English dictionary translated "tract" as an "admonishing the world text" (*quanshiwen*), likely reflecting Liang's influence: Robert Henry Mathews, Minyuan Wang, and Yuen Ren Chao, *Mathews' Chinese-English Dictionary: A Chinese English Dictionary Compiled for the China Inland Mission,* rev. American ed. (Cambridge: Harvard University Press, 1931; reprint, 1996), 235. This dictionary is often described as a "missionary dictionary" and was associated with the China Inland Mission.

19. Ryan Dunch drew my attention to an analogy with *secular/worldly,* which are English terms that also convey a connection between time and geography.

20. P. Richard Bohr, "Jesus, Christianity and Rebellion in China," in Roman Malek, ed., *The Chinese Face of Jesus Christ,* vol. 2, 621–22.

21. Ibid., 613–61.

22. Daniel Overmyer writes about the "precious volumes" *baojuan* tradition that is sometimes seen as including "morality books." Daniel L. Overmyer, *Precious Volumes: An Introduction to Chinese Sectarian Scriptures from the Sixteenth and Seventeenth Centuries*

(Cambridge: Harvard University Asia Center, distributed by Harvard University Press, 1999).

23. Cynthia J. Brokaw, *The Ledgers of Merit and Demerit: Social Change and Moral Order in Late Imperial China* (Princeton: Princeton University Press, 1991), 3.

24. Philip Kuhn in Twichett and Fairbank, eds., *Cambridge History of China*, vol. 10, *Late Ch'ing, 1800–1811, Part 1* (Cambridge: Cambridge University Press, 1978), 267.

25. Ibid.

26. Alexander Wylie, *Memorials of Protestant Missionaries to the Chinese: Giving a List of Their Publications, and Obituary Notices of the Deceased, with Copious Indexes* (Shanghae: American Presbyterian Mission Press, 1867), 23, notes that a theme of *Good News* Chapter 3 is "redeeming sin to save the world" *dai shu zui jiushi.*

27. Thomas Reilly, *The Taiping Heavenly Kingdom,* 64.

28. Ibid. He goes so far as to say that "Liang's tract was nothing but a collection of Morrison's translated scripture, mostly appearing without any commentary or explanation of the contents, making a discussion of matters outside a narrowly conceived religious sphere unnecessary."

29. Ibid., 65.

30. Ibid., 65.

31. Jonathan Seitz, "Review Essay of Thomas Harvey's *Acquainted with Grief: Wang Mingdao's Stand for the Persecuted Church in China;* and Thomas Reilly's *The Taiping Heavenly Kingdom: Rebellion and the Blasphemy of Empire," Koinonia Journal* 17/1 (2005) 105–9.

32. One of the two works included in Andrew West's catalogue *by* Morrison is his translation of the book of Exodus, *Chu Maixiguo Zhuan.* West, *Catalogue of the Morrison Collection of Chinese Books* (London: University of London School of Oriental and African Studies, 1998), 237, 350.

33. Princeton Theological Seminary Special Collections has a single chapter of *Good News.* There is no indication it was ever included in a larger work, and it is probable that chapters were handed out individually.

34. Asceticism and discipline are key themes in Max Weber, *The Protestant Ethic and the Spirit of Capitalism* (Penguin Twentieth-Century Classics; New York: Penguin, 2002). Weber traced the development of asceticism through monasticism into a broader society where laypeople emphasize a life of work, thrift, and public piety. William James, *The Varieties of Religious Experience* (New York: Vintage, 1990), presented an understanding of conversion as practiced; however, virtually all of his examples were drawn from working-class American and British evangelical conversions. The accounts typically portrayed singular events modeled off a common cultural understanding of experiential conversion.

35. Alexander Wylie, *Memorials of Protestant Missionaries to the Chinese,* 23–24. The content of the chapters is described as (1) "A true Account of the salvation of Mankind" including the creation account and the polemic against Chinese religion, described below; (2) "Following the True and rejecting the False"; (3) "A collection of various Tracts"; (4) "Miscellaneous explanations of Holy Scriptures"; (5) "Miscellaneous statements

founded on the Holy Scriptures"; (6) "Perfect Acquaintance with the true Doctrine"; (7) "On obtaining Happiness whether in Peace or Peril"; (8) "Excellent sayings from the true Scriptures"; and (9) "Selections from the ancient Scriptures."

36. Ibid., 24–25. These are both part of Harvard's microfilmed collection of Chinese Protestant works: Liang Fa, *Jian xuan quan shi yao yan* [*"Selections from Good News to Admonish the Ages"*] (Singapore: Jian xia shu yuan cang ban, [1830s]) ; Liang Fa, *Qiu Fu Mian Huo Yao Lun* [*"Important Discourse on Seeking Happiness and Escaping Misery"*] (Singapore: Jian xia shu yuan cang ban, [1830s]). These books are reasonably catalogued as appearing in the 1830s, although an exact date is not fixed upon.

37. Whalen Lai, "The First Chinese Christian Gospel," 90.

38. Conversion was the major topic of my dissertation (note 9), but an article based on the thesis has appeared: Jonathan A. Seitz, "Is Conversion to Christianity Pantheon Theocide? Fragility and Durability in Early Diasporic Chinese Protestantism," in Richard Fox Young and Jonathan A. Seitz, eds., *Asia in the Making of Christianity: Conversion, Agency, and Indigeneity, 1600s to the Present* (Social Sciences in Asia 35; Leiden: Brill, 2013), 153–87.

39. George McNeur, *China's First Preacher*, 37 [this edition, p. 35].

40. Ibid [this edition, p. 35].

41. Ibid [this edition, p. 36].

42. Elizabeth Morrison, *Memoirs of the Life and Labours of Robert Morrison, D.D.* (London: Longman, Orme, Brown, Green, and Longmans, 1889), 2:225.

43. Ibid.

44. Ibid.

45. Whalen Lai, "The First Chinese Christian Gospel," 91, identifies a church-sect split (as in Weber and Troeltsch), but any group consisting of two or three missionaries and only a couple of converts would have been sectarian.

46. "Essays, Missionary Fragments, &c.," *Indo-Chinese Gleaner* 2:12 (4/1820) 327. At this point there were only two converts, and we know Liang had a father.

47. Medhurst, *China: Its State and Prospects with Especial Reference to the Spread of the Gospel; Containing Allusions to the Antiquity, Extent, Population, Civilization, Literature, and Religion of the Chinese* (Boston: Crocker & Brewster, 1838), 272.

48. Liang Fa, *Good News*, 305. The book's title in pinyin is *Jiushi lu cuoyaolüe jie*.

49. Ibid.

50. Ibid., 306.

51. Nancy E. Park, "Corruption in Eighteenth-Century China," *Journal of Asian Studies* 56/4 (1997) 970, distinguishes two types of crimes, public crimes (*gongzui*) or private crimes (*sizui*).

52. Liang Fa, *Good News*, 306.

53. Elizabeth Morrison, *Life and Labours of Robert Morrison*, 2:38

54. Ibid., 38, 58, 224, 432, 449.

55. Su Ching, *The Printing Presses of the London Missionary Society among the Chinese,* 67, citing LMS, SC, 2.1. B. Morrison to Burder, Canton, 14 November 1819, 2.1.C., ibid., Canton, 26 November 1819. The character here should be Romanized in Wade-Giles as *tsuo.*

56. Alexander Wylie, *Memorials of Protestant Missionaries to the Chinese,* 22: "37 leaves. Canton, 1819. This contains a preface concerning God as the Creator, and object of worship, to which the ten commandments are attached—passages in 2nd Chapter of the Hebrews—2 Peter, 2nd chapter—whole of the 1st chapter, part of the 2nd, 3rd and 4th of James, explained—2 Timothy 3:15—1 Peter 3:10 to the end—1 Peter 4:3 to 10— 1 John 1:8, 9—James 5th—three hymns and prayers. As the composition of a Christian Chinese mechanic, who was totally unacquainted with the gospel six years before, this tract cannot be expected to display a deep acquaintance with theology; but it appears on the whole evangelical, serious, and useful. It was first submitted to Dr. Morrison, and having obtained his approval, A-fa printed 200 copies for distribution. While thus engaged, he was carried off to prison, and the blocks and books seized and burnt by the police officers." Since the book and blocks were burned, it is not clear where Wylie obtained this information.

57. Cited in George McNeur, *China's First Preacher,* 36 [this edition, pp. 34–35].

58. Elizabeth Morrison, *Memoirs of the Life and Labours of Robert Morrison,* vol. 2, 235.

59. Liang Fa, *Good News,* 309.

60. Elizabeth Morrison, *Memoirs of the Life and Labours of Robert Morrison,* vol. 2, 235.

61. George McNeur, *China's First Preacher,* 41 [this edition, p. 42].

62. Elizabeth Morrison, *Memoirs of the Life and Labours of Robert Morrison,* vol. 2, 357.

62. Ibid., 358.

64. Walter Medhurst, *China: Its State and Prospects,* 271. It is unclear why or how Medhurst includes the additional comment. Did Elizabeth Morrison redact Medhurst's account in her edition of her husband's memoirs, or did one or the other have independent access to Liang's original Chinese document?

65. Liang Fa, *Good News,* 22–43. The pinyin, *Lun shiren mihuo yu ge shen fo pusa zhi lei. Pusa,* can be translated variously as "Bodhisattva," "Buddhist image/idol," or "benevolent/kind being."

66. This polemic is also included in the shorter selection based on *Good News* that Liang wrote: *Jian xuan quan shi yao yan* ["*Selections from Good News to Admonish the Ages*"].

67. Liang Fa, *Good News,* 24.

68. Ibid., 25.

69. Ibid., 26–27.

70. In fairness, this may be something he worked out with the missionaries. While I did not find the four term names for God in early missionary writing, they did use the

phrase *Shengtian* ("Divine Heavenly") in writing about the Scriptures. Liang, however, seems to be unique in using four-word names for all three persons of the trinity.

71. On Chinese Bible translations see Thor Strandenaes, *Principles of Chinese Bible Translation: As Expressed in Five Selected Versions of the New Testament and Exemplified by Mt 5:1–12 and Col 1* (Stockholm: Almqvist & Wiksell, 1987), and Jost Oliver Zetzsche, *The Bible in China: The History of the Union Version, or, the Culmination of Protestant Missionary Bible Translation in China* (Sankt Augustin: Monumenta Serica Institute, 1999).

72. Reilly, *The Taiping Heavenly Kingdom*, 22, 101–3, 157. Terms for Jesus in LMS writing included a longer name "Jesus Christ" (*Jilishidu*) and the transliteration of "messiah," *Mishiya*.

73. Andrew Walls, *The Cross-Cultural Process in Christian History* (Maryknoll: Orbis, 2002), 79–80. Walls writes about how early Greek Christians, for whom the word *messiah* "meant nothing," quickly "chose the word *Kyrios*, 'Lord,' the title that Greek pagans used for their cult divinities (Acts 11:19–21)." That Christians in China chose terms like *lord, savior,* or *son of God* thus shows that they found local words that were viable possibilities to describe Jesus.

74. The choice of names was not without controversy. Popular candidates included *Tianzhu* ("Lord of Heaven"), *Shangdi* ("Lord on High"), and *Shen* ("god," "spirit").

75. Liang Fa, *Good News*, 25, 134, 162, 352. Examples include "Chinese people" (*Zhongguo zhi ren*) "China's three teachings: Ruism, Buddhism, and Daoism" (*Zhongguo Ru, Shi, Dao sanjiao zhe*) "far from our China" (*Li women Zhongguo yaoyuan*), and "my China has the way of sagely benevolence and righteousness" (*Wo Zhongguo you le shengxian renyi zhi dadao*).

76. Alexander Wylie, *Memorials of Protestant Missionaries to the Chinese*, 79–80. Williams and Ira Tracy left with the ABCFM for China, arriving in 1833. Ira Tracy graduated from Andover Seminary and arrived in China in 1832. Both works listed are in the Harvard Collection: *Yapian su gai wen* and *Xinjiapo zaizhonghui gaosu zhongguo zuochan zhi ren*.

77. Jonathan Spence, *God's Chinese Son*, 62, citing Liang, *Good News*, 88, 96.

78. Frank Dikötter et al., *Narcotic Culture: A History of Drugs in China* (Chicago: University of Chicago Press, 2004), 100.

79. Diana Carroll, "Contribution of the Malacca Missionaries and *The Hikayat Abdullah*," in Kwame Sundaram Jomo, ed., *Rethinking Malaysia* (Malaysian Studies 1; Kuala Lumpur: Malaysian Social Science Association, 1999), 151.

80. Jessie Lutz, "A Profile of Chinese Protestant Evangelists," in *Authentic Chinese Christianity: Preludes to Its Development (Nineteenth and Twentieth Centuries)*, ed. Ku W`ei-ying and Koen De Ridder (Leuven Chinese Studies 9; Leuven: Leuven University Press, 2001), 80.

Editor's Notes on This Edition

To render the volume more legible, I have used optical character recognition software to reproduce the text, and have tried to improve photo quality. For this reprinted volume, I cite known works for quotations and sometimes offer additional information about people or events mentioned. (Many of the works McNeur cites are now in the public domain and can be found easily in electronic databases.) McNeur sometimes made minor changes to quotes to improve readability or explain obscure references. I also have updated older English spellings or small errata, and included a table listing Chinese words romanized in the text, along with the corresponding characters and pinyin romanization.

I am grateful to Mrs. Margaret Moore, the oldest living descendant of McNeur's. In addition to granting permission for the project, she also provided helpful biographical data and information. I owe the greatest debt of gratitude to Carol Hamrin, Wright Doyle, and the editors at Pickwick Publicatons. They showed exceptional patience; I began the project in Princeton with one child and finish it now in Taipei with three. In developing a series on Chinese Christianity, and supporting it through close reading and editing, Carol, Wright, and Pickwick Publications provide a genuine service. It is fitting that they have chosen to include the work of the earliest Chinese Protestant printer and editor, Liang Fa. I hope this edition honors his work. All remaining mistakes are my own.

Jonathan A. Seitz

Foreword

It was a fine day in South China a few years ago. A group of Church representatives from many parts of China met in the great city of Canton for a Church conference. One afternoon they assembled before the tomb of the man whose life story is given in this little book. A service was held, a tree planted, in commemoration of this man of God. As they stood around the grave of LIANG A-FA their hearts were deeply moved and stirred. Their minds went back to the early days of the Christian Movement first in China, then the Roman world in the first century. The connection of these lines of thought was both natural and vital. For Liang's life and work was but an additional chapter of the history of the Christian Church, a continuation of the Book of Acts of the Apostles. This simple biography clearly teaches us that the foundation of the Christian Church is well and solidly laid in the heart of men in the Orient; that the saving power of God is the same yesterday, today and forever; and what God can do in, with, for and through even one man when his life is wholly devoted and consecrated to Him and His work.

We are indebted to the author of the book for his painstaking work in collecting the data and assembling the material, probably both not in great abundance, so that we may catch some glimpse not so much of the achievement of the man but the power of his Master in whose name and for whose sake he lived and labored. We hope and pray that LIANG A-FA though dead may yet speak to us through these pages and thereby rekindle in our souls the holy fire for the evangelization of the world at such a time of universal unrest which is so far reaching and challenging.

C. Y. Cheng.[1]
Shanghai, 1934.

Notes

1. Cheng Chingyi (1881–1939) was a major Chinese Christian leader who was one of three Chinese representatives at the 1910 World Missionary Conference in Edinburgh, for ten years (1924–1934) secretary of the National Christian Council, and then (in 1934) secretary of Church of Christ in China. See Daniel Bays, "Ch'eng Ching-Yi (Cheng Chingyi), 130, in Gerald Anderson, ed., *Biographical Dictionary of Christian Missions* (New York: Simon & Schuster Macmillan, 1998).

Preface

The Rev. T. W. Pearce, LL.D., veteran missionary of the London Missionary Society in South China, pays the following tribute to the subject of this memoir:

"To faith and patience carried to the plane of the martyr there was added versatility of gifts and graces that rendered Liang A-fa one of the greater forerunners of a type—still the 'leading' type in churches and missions—which translates Christianity thoroughly and in its essence into Chinese life, and uses every gift and grace for its diffusion."

"He is an example of the class that Christianity uplifts, ennobles, and fits for a kind of service to the church and to the world that only becomes possible to the man of vigorous independent mind who is led from strength to strength by the power of the Unseen and through the indwelling of the Holy Spirit."

Dr. Pearce is undoubtedly right in finding the open secret of Liang A-fa's character and service in the reality and intensity of his devotional life. His familiarity with Scripture, the simple directness of his prayers, the fearlessness of his witness, and the saintliness of his character carry us right back to their one source in Christ Himself. No wonder Professor Harlan P. Beach wrote of him "Liang A-fa would count as a host in any age."

G. H. McN
Canton, China, November 1933.
Shanghai, 1934.

1

The Light of Sacred Story

"It is one of my deepest convictions that all over the world, and possibly nowhere more than back in the Western countries themselves, we need to institute as never before the study of church history . . . I honestly believe that we are headed into the most difficult time in the history of our religion, and we need to treasure greatly the lessons of the centuries. I have great confidence in the study of Christianity, ecumenical Christianity, and above all vital Christianity."[1]

—DR. J. R. MOTT

Much has been written—although not enough—about the missionary pioneers of Protestant Christianity in China. But the story of the expansion of our Christian religion as it has spread over the wide world during the centuries cannot be complete without the record of those sons of the soil—the first fruits of China and other lands unto Christ—who were won by the pioneers, and became in their turn the earliest heralds of Christ to their kinsmen. Here we are in touch with vital Christianity in its most evident, and effective expression Just as in the Acts of the Apostles and its continued narrative through the history of the early Church we find satisfying proof of Christ's power to redeem and transform mankind, so in every fresh Christian conquest in a new field this faith has fuller confirmation, and evangelistic zeal gathers added inspiration. The life stories of trophies won from the thralldom of ignorant, superstitious, and debasing beliefs, and changed into saintly, self-sacrificing, and loving servants of God and man, bring renewed tribute to the supremacy of our Lord and unite diadems of other rich tints with His many crowns. In these days of fuller historical knowledge, wider charity, and deeper understanding of Christ, we are more ready than our forefathers to admit the values existing in the partial and often misleading conceptions of truth presented in non-Christian religions. Master builders like Robert Morrison found certain materials ready to their hand when they began their task. God had never left Himself without a witness in the hearts of His Chinese children. The ancient classical literature of China contained ideas of God and human duty expressed in terms which such pioneers did not hesitate to use when introducing the more perfect Divine revelation. In the modified form of Buddhism they found in possession of China's religious instincts, there were certain features which almost seemed to indicate Christian influence in its far past. Along with Taoism it had at least kept faith in the world of spirit alive in the hearts of the common people. And Protestants should never forget that for centuries the Roman Church, often in spite of bitterest persecution, had been teaching throughout China the Gospel of the Cross. Dr. Morrison's first language teacher after arrival was a Catholic Christian, and he used the earlier work of some unknown Jesuit priest as a help in his translation of the New Testament.[2] But while the Protestant pioneers gratefully utilized what the past had provided for the new day of opportunity, they never questioned the unique supremacy of Jesus Christ, nor compromised with anything that contradicted His teaching as they understood it. If they had, they would not have been Protestant pioneers. And it is natural that the characters of the men and women whom they won for Christ—the first generation of disciples—should witness to their spiritual lineage, both near and distant. There could be no better example than Liang A-fa, the subject of this biography. He was a real Chinese and a real Christian.

Robert Morrison died at Canton, China, on the first day of August in 1834, almost a century ago. At such a time it is appropriate that we not only study afresh the character and work of that noble missionary, but that we remember also the Chinese colleague to whom he then bequeathed the care of the infant church gathered under his ministry. That early transference of responsibility should have its lessons for us in these days when varying causes are forcing a somewhat questioning but yet rapid devolution from foreign to Chinese control. It will prove that by every token the Chinese Church has always had her own leaders who were in the true apostolic succession. The combined study should shed light on the contribution that Christianity in China most needs from the older church, as well as what this young church has to share with her sisters elsewhere. A senior Y.M.C.A.

secretary from America said to his capable Chinese colleagues at Canton some years ago, "You can do without us now. You know far better how to run a Chinese Y.M.C.A. than we do." "Yes", replied the Chinese general secretary, "we know how to run the 'Y' but we need you for character." This biography should help us appreciate the fact that we of differing races united in Christ need each other for character.

Interest in China's church history requires quickening. Data regarding the foreign mission side may be carefully preserved in the archives of mission boards and research libraries. But the biographer of a Chinese life is heavily handicapped. So little relevant material has withstood the ravages of time. Such an experience makes one grateful that the scene of early church history was in a favorable climate for the preservation of written records, and that the writers used durable material. The rubbish heaps outside old Chinese cities will never reward the historian in the same way as those of Western Asia. In the climate of South China the difficulties of keeping written and printed data are multiplied. If it is true in other lands that once a life of biographical worth has been completed by death the sooner it is written the better, such a maxim has special cogency in Kwangtung. Termites have an abnormal taste for literature, as many a missionary has found to his cost. Borers, bookworms, silver-fish, cockroaches, mould, and other pests take their toll. The humidity of the climate reduces paper to its original pulp, and devastating floods are of frequent occurrence. In the summer of 1915 the Canton delta region suffered such an inundation. At Liang A-fa's old home on Honam near Canton there was stored a basket of papers and books left there by him when he died sixty years before. A Christian relative, realizing that these might include documents of historic value, took the basket in a boat to a Christian institution in the city. But just then the old building occupied by the institution was being pulled down and a new one erected. Storage accommodation was limited, and there was no one present who sensed the importance of the situation. The basket was returned to its former corner, the climbing waters covered its contents, and no one knows how much—or how little—the Chinese church lost of its first evangelist's life story. A few family portraits—among them one of Liang A-fa, some worm-eaten papers, and a time-worn copy of St. Matthew's Gospel printed at Canton in 1813, are all that can be found. Even the genealogical record of the family, although the custom of ancestral worship has made the preservation of such data universal in China, is difficult to trace. So far as is known not a single copy of the many tracts written by the evangelist has been discovered.[3] The young Chinese church must take timely warning, and make suitable arrangements for the collection and preservation of the facts relating to its history. Much has already been irrevocably lost. Recent visits to China by American specialists in church history have awakened a new interest, and Chinese church leaders are beginning to develop a keener sense of historic values.

Another reason for the lack of worthwhile biographical material in China is that Chinese standards of biographical record have been set in a stereotyped mould which robs them of any human interest. Dr. Robert Morrison wrote "In the larger histories of China biographical notices of eminent persons are introduced, but they are generally mere skeletons. Like a great deal of Chinese history there is nothing but bone, no flesh and skin to beautify the body. The name of a person, when born, where he lived, what offices he held, and when he died, made up a biography." True we have heard something the same about textbooks on history in English. A medical friend told me that when on a health furlough in Japan and ordered to take a sleep every afternoon he found an unfailing soporific in a well-known but old-fashioned text-book on Church History. That something much more interesting is possible to Chinese writers has abundant proof in the many popular dramas like "The Three Kingdoms," where imagination has been allowed to play around the scanty historical data until the dead past has lived again for the millions of people who through succeeding generations have never tired of its comedy and tragedy. Something of this art, although more closely related to sober fact, is needed today by the Chinese church historian. His work will then find a wide and interested audience. At a time of accentuated racial consciousness things Chinese are worth much just because they are Chinese. The demand for an "indigenous" church turns attention to what makes it "indigenous." And when one looks on the spreading branches of this tree, the flowers and fruit of which are increasingly beautifying and enriching the new life of this old land, the question as to the seed from which it grew takes us back to this pioneer Chinese evangelist who, through lonely, long, and fiery testing, evidenced the strength and sincerity of his faith.

Fortunately we are not altogether without written Chinese data. In the archives of the London Missionary Society in London there is an original letter, still in its Chinese envelope, written by Liang A-fa in 1827.[4] Along with it there is a journal written by the evangelist between March 28 and November 6, 1830.[5] These valuable documents were courteously sent to

Canton for six months, and the greatest surprise was expressed by the Chinese who saw them so well preserved in spite of the century that had past since they were penned. Surviving relatives have provided a few meager details which have come down to them. For the rest English material has been sought in many directions and found in a few. Original letters by Dr. Morrison and Milne and Dr. Hobson to their Mission Board have been gone through by friends and relevant material copied out. Enough has been gathered to sketch the portrait of one whom the church should place in its hall of fame. He might have been lost to us altogether. Yet in a book published in London during 1846 Liang A-fa is mentioned with the remark "Nothing concerning him need be said here, as his praise is in all the churches."[6] The first Bishop of Victoria, Hong Kong, Rev. George Smith, could write of him as "well-known by name in Europe and America."[7] In 1841 part of his story was told by Dr. Peter Parker before the Senate and House of Representatives of the United States. His name appeared in the report of a commission presented to the British House of Commons in 1847. The Chinese have a proverb "Even the crab in a pond without fish is considered big" and it may be argued that the only Chinese Protestant evangelist would naturally attract attention in Christian countries. This story should effectively answer that argument. Whatever the reasons, his name has been gradually forgotten. A few years ago even the church in China knew nothing of him. A strange coincidence led to his grave being discovered on the outskirts of Canton in 1918. Interest in the pioneer began to revive. A Chinese biography published in 1930 was the result of that awakened interest.[8] The story is told again in English in response to many requests, and with the conviction that Liang A-fa should be reinstated to the honored place he once held in the estimation of Christians in Europe and America.

Notes

1. National Christian Council of China, *Conference on the Church in China Today* (Shanghai: China Press, 1926), 43–44.

2. This is now known to be the Jean Basset manuscript. Copies exist as the British Museum, the Hong Kong Bible Society, and elsewhere. On Basset, see Jost Zetzsche, *The Bible in China: The History of the Union Version, or, the Culmination of Protestant Missionary Bible Translation in China* (Sankt Augustin: Monumenta Serica Institute, 1999), 37–38.

3. See the introduction (above) for works that have surfaced since George McNeur's time, including the nine-chapter *Good News to Admonish the Ages* and several smaller tracts.

4. This is part of the Church World Mission collection which has been microfilmed by the company IDC. The original collection exists in the library of the School of Oriental and African Studies in London.

5. Ibid.

6. Evan Davies, *Memoir of the Rev. Samuel Dyer, Sixteen Year Missionary to the Chinese* (London: John Snow, 1846), 205.

7. George Smith, *A Narrative of an Exploratory Visit to Each of the Consular cities of China and to the Islands of Hong Kong and Chusan in Behalf of the Church Missionary Society in the Years 1844, 1845, 1846* (New York: Harper & Brothers, 1857), 11.

8. George Hunter McNeur, *Zhonghua zui zao de bu dao zhe Liang Fa* (Shanghai: Guang xue hui, 1931).

2

The Making of a Prophet

"The book of life has no preface. Every page is a page of the real story, and it has some essential line in it if only we can find it."

—PERCY AINSWORTH[1]

The district of Koming (Lofty Clearness) is one of the smaller units of the Kwangtung province, and is overshadowed by the importance of its surrounding neighbors. Apart from the walled district city the best-known market town is Samchow (Three Islands) so-called because there are three islands in the river beside it. Within half an hour's journey from that market you can enter any one of three other districts. Such border towns and the adjacent country have traditionally a bad name in China. It was so easy for bands of robbers to move from one district to the other and thus escape pursuit by district officers who were afraid to follow them into another magistracy. Jealousy between neighboring officials also increased the freedom of these outlaws. With unified military control conditions are now peaceful, but any trouble which leads to a temporary withdrawal of the local garrison leaves the way open for a return to the robbery and piracy so prevalent whenever opportunity offers. On the opposite side of the river from the town of Samchow is the village of Lohtsun (probably named after some historic person). Here Liang A-fa was born in 1789, the fifty-third year in the long reign of Emperor Kien Lung. The biographer of the Rev. Wm. Milne, D.D., begins his book with the words "If Liang A-fa possess any susceptibility he could not witness unmoved, nor unprofited, the scenery of Kennetmont in Scotland, where Wm. Milne, his spiritual father, followed the ewes."[2] There is little to move the spectator in the scenery around Liang A-fa's own birthplace. The village is in the centre of a low-lying plain with distant hills surrounding it. So low is the country that flood-dykes are the only means of communication with neighboring villages. The town of Samchow is built along a flood bank which makes it what the Scotch would call "a lang toon." Heavy rain during the summer months raises the level of the river above the rice- fields on either side, and so the intricate system of dykes is necessary. Just as a ship is divided into various water-tight compartments the banks are built so that a breach in one may not affect too wide an area. But occasionally abnormal rainfalls swell the river and its subsidiary canals to such an extent that all the low fields and villages are inundated, causing extensive loss and suffering. In a district subject to calamities of this nature the sequence of events in local history is related to one or other of these disastrous floods. Throughout the rice-growing area in the Canton delta there are many parts where danger of flood in summer is so constant that no crop is planted in the spring, but only in late summer when the risk is passed. On the higher ground two crops annually are the rule. Around Liang A-fa's village the fields are so low that the water seldom entirely leaves them. In some cases they cannot even be ploughed or harrowed, but fertilizer is cast on the water and the rice planted in the soft mud. This can only be done, however, when the water is not too deep, as the plants will die if completely submerged for any length of time. The seed is first sown in a small rich plot, and when the rice is six inches or more high, bunches of plants are placed in a tub which the farmer pushes before him as he puts in his crop in regular rows. Difficult and precarious conditions of livelihood affected the villagers in ways which are typically exemplified in the story of Liang A-fa.

Coming to an area subject to flood, the original settlers naturally looked for higher land on which to build their homes, and Lohtsun is the result of a careful quest, being scattered over a series of little hills, and divided into wards according to the clan names of its inhabitants. The Liang clan is in the front of the village, which is the West ward, and the houses are on the lower slopes, and at the foot of a rocky hill about fifty feet in height. On the top are great banyan trees, the bastard banyan which has the usual aerial roots of its species, but which, instead of taking root and forming new trees, tends rather to cover the original trunk with a network of ridges, adding considerably to its size. Under the shade of these wide spreading branches A-fa played and rested as a child. Perhaps he too, like the boy in the Chinese version of "The Atheist and the Acorn," wondered why the Creator had given this giant tree its tiny berries, while the trailing vine produced such mighty pumpkins. And perhaps he got the same answer to the puzzle when the tap of a little berry on his face woke him from sleep under its leafy canopy. In front of the hamlet stands the Liang ancestral temple, where the spirit tablets of the family are enshrined and worshipped. On one side rises a strongly built watch-tower, with its heavily-barred windows and iron door. Many of A-fa's youthful experiences must have centered round this guard-house when he listened to the drum and gong of the watch-man, or saw the hurried assembly of the village guards when the alarm was sounded. That whole region was the scene of frequent wars between the Punteis and the Hakkas, the Punteis being the Cantonese-speaking inhabitants and the Hakkas, (lit. strangers) a tribe which came from North China many centuries ago and is now scattered over a great part of South China.[3] The struggle between them was for the possession of the fertile plains. Finally strength of numbers enabled the Punteis to drive the Hakkas back to the hills, where they still have their village homes. This building was also used as a place of refuge in time of flood by the villagers living on the lower levels. In A-fa's boyhood days that high tower must have been alive with stories of peril and escape which would make vividly real to him in later Christian experience many of the Psalmists' references to such a place of refuge. Vegetable gardens, mulberry plots, with occasional patches of tobacco plant and hemp, are found on the higher ground among the houses. Along the straggling flood dykes the boys and girls herd the water buffaloes and cattle.

Amid such surroundings Liang A-fa was born and bred. The house in which he first saw the light of day has disappeared, but on its site, in a narrow back lane, there still stands the dwelling built by the evangelist when his house was swept away by a flood in 1833. The wooden beams are rotting, the brick walls are beginning to crumble, and one fears what may happen to the decrepit old man who finds shelter under its roof. But, however desolate the house is today, there was great joy in the home of Liang Ch'ung-nang away back in 1789 when a man child was born into the world. The proud father little dreamed that this tiny tot was to play so strange a part in his nation's history. He called him "Fa" ("Faat" in Cantonese) one of the common meanings of which is "sent."[4] Chinese parents, like the ancient Hebrews, always have a reason for the choice of a son's name. They may have hoped this son was sent to bring wealth and glory to the clan. According to the Chinese traditional view not only was that hope unrealized but the very opposite happened. But the name recalls to the Christian the words "There was a man sent from God."[5] The affix "A" commonly preceding the name "Fa" is added in Cantonese for the sake of euphony to names which consist of only one word or of which only one word is familiarly used. The family was poor, which explains the fact that A-fa was eleven years old before he went to school. They had the characteristic ambition for their son, or at that age he would not have been sent to school at all. As he grew up he took his part in the duties of domestic and farm life—running errands, gathering fuel, herding ducks, geese, pigs or cattle. Doubtless these years were full of character-forming influences and incidents which had their sequel in the struggles and conquests of maturer life. We have no written record of them. He was learning to live. "There are no unrecorded years. The pen of the historian may be idle but for all that the history is written. It is graven in character. At the end a man's character stands the abiding product of all his deeds and all his days." There is no stage at which the clay of human life is so susceptible to molding influences as in early youth.

It must have taken some courage for a lad of eleven to begin his education in the school, meeting then as now in the ancestral temple. Chinese boys as a rule start schooling several years earlier. He would thus be in the same class with much younger children. But he would be more developed than they, and better able to profit by his belated opportunity. The earnest desire for knowledge indicated is so typical of the Chinese that it is not unusual to find such cases even now, when the school system is being modernized. A historian has told us the main direction of A-fa's studies. We would have known them anyway because centuries saw no variation in the old classical schools. He began with the Three Character Classic, the trimetrical primer compiled over a thousand years ago.[6] In its pages filial and fraternal duties are inculcated by precept and example. It lauds the virtue of diligence in the pursuit of knowledge thus: "To vanquish sleep one suspended his head by the hair from a beam, and another pierced his thigh with an awl. One read by light of glow-worms, another by reflection of light from the snow. Though their families were poor these did not forget to study. One carried faggots, and another tied his books to the horn of an ox. While thus engaged in labor they studied with intensity."[7] During his four years at school he also committed to memory the Four Books, the Five Classics, and the Sacred Edict, the two former sets being the ancient

Confucian classics and the last a series of moral maxims written by the second emperor of the Manchu dynasty.[8] Thus A-fa gained at least a nodding acquaintance with the rich classical lore of his race, and laid the literary foundations without which his life work would have been impossible. One thing he certainly learned to do well. That was to write with care and correctness the intricate Chinese characters. The letter from his brush still lying in the archives of the L.M.S. in London bears witness to that fact, and is a striking testimony both to the ability of the teacher and the diligence of the pupil. This introduction to the lofty ethical principles of Confucianism and the hoary wisdom of the sages, along with the training received in courtesy and self-control, all bore fruit in after years. And every morning the pupil bowed before the shrine of Confucius as well as to the teacher before taking his seat at his desk. The soul tablets of his ancestors—a great cloud of witnesses looked down upon him from the rear of the temple.

So far nothing has been said of the mother. When Liang A-fa wrote some of his religious experiences years later he mentions his early devotion to Buddhism. That was something he "drank in with his mother's milk" as Bengel says of Timothy. Even as a babe borne on mother's back in the carrying-band to the temple of the Goddess of Mercy, he would be taught to put his little hands together and bow his head at her shrine. He learned to worship before the scrolls, altars, and idols each new and full moon with incense sticks, candles, fire crackers and paper money. When the tombs of ancestors were visited each year he shared in the joyous reverence of the festival. Thus the deeply religious nature so evident in the earnest evangelist was developed in its earliest stages by the worship of the home, the school and the temple. These were his tutors, however stubbornly he might himself have disputed the fact, and in spite of their mistakes and imperfections, to lead him towards Christ. The fresh visions and sacred experiences of his new faith were, deep down in his subconsciousness, rooted in the permanent elements of his early religious life. The truth of this would only be questioned by those who had not known the difficulty of making any spiritual impression on such young Chinese of today as are the product of worshipless homes and secular schools. Earnest pagans make the best Christians. We recall Wordsworth's preference for the faith of "a pagan suckled in a creed outworn" when he thought of the visionless worldlings around him.[9]

Another proof of the family poverty is furnished in the fact that at fifteen A-fa left his village home to seek work in the city of Canton. A yet more certain proof is that he went unmarried. If it had been possible to scrape together, or borrow on good security, the money necessary to buy a bride, the home would not have been left without a daughter- in-law to serve the mother. Chinese village life has little attraction for young lads. Apart from farming or work of some kind in a neighboring market there is little choice of occupation, and so the city has always exercised a strong pull on the more independent and venturesome of Chinese youth. The young men of Lohtsun still seek elsewhere the money needed to support the children, women, and older folk left in the village. We can picture the lad leaving his boyhood home and wending his way along the top of the dykes towards Samchow and the passage boat. He carries his few clothes rolled in a cotton quilt and covered with a straw mat. It is the year 1804, but because some things are timeless, we can guess there is a package of home-made cakes in A-fa's luggage, and that it was with a tear in his eye that he took his last look back at the village, with its trees and tower and temple, before boarding the ship for Canton. His mother would not sleep much that night, for such is the way of mothers.

Under a broad matting sail when the wind was favorable, and by towing, poling and rowing when it was contrary, the broad flat-bottomed junk, now through narrow canals, and again on the great river, travelled towards the city. Next day as it crept up the Macao Reach past the Teetotum Forts, Liang A-fa got his first glimpse of Canton, and at the same time his first contact with the wider world. For there along the foreshore stood the row of foreign factories, the flags of many nations flying from their high masts. These were known as the "Shih-san Hong" or thirteen hong, "hong" designating a row of buildings. The English word "factory" indicated the residence of "factors," or agents for the purchase and sale of merchandise. Each series of buildings had its own distinctive name both in English and Chinese, and ran from the foreshore right through the whole block. Built of brick or granite, and two or three stories high, they presented a very sub- stantial front, and immediately attracted the attention of visiting strangers. The Chinese lad little thought he would later be a familiar visitor among these hated and despised foreign barbarians. For many years the passage- boat from Samchow has moored just below the former site of the foreign factories, and it is not unlikely that A-fa landed at the same spot over a cen- tury ago. At that time there was no Protestant missionary in China, but in the same year young Robert Morrison sent his application for service to the London Missionary Society with the prayer "that God would station him in that part of the missionary field where the difficulties were the greatest and to all human appearance the most insurmountable."[10] That prayer was certainly answered when he was appointed to China.

A-fa found work with a maker of Chinese brush pens, but very soon left this occupation and apprenticed himself to an engraver of wooden printing blocks. Printing from wooden blocks had been known in China from the beginning of the seventh century, and was used by Imperial order in reproducing the classics during 952 AD. The wood used was cut into small slabs about the size of a foolscap sheet of paper and an inch or less thick. The book to be printed was written out most carefully by a good writer in the square form of the characters used in books, and then pasted face downwards on the block. The block cutter rubbed off the paper with his wet finger leaving the ink impression on the wood. Then, with various graving tools according to the nature of the work to be done, and using a wooden mallet, he cut away, to the depth of about a quarter of an inch, all the surface of the wood not covered by the writing, thus leaving the characters in relief. Sometimes both surfaces of the blocks were utilized. A-fa continued this work for four years under the same master. Week by week throughout these years the young workman became more adept. Not only was he learning the trade which made him most useful in the earliest stages of Christian work in China, but he was continuously adding to his knowledge of Chinese literature, and thus preparing for the higher task of author and preacher. All unconscious to himself and others the apprentice was being trained by another Master for His own service. When God of old chose a prophet, the endowment of his whole nature, his physical and moral environment, all the influences of heredity and education that had shaped his life and made him what he was, worked together under the Divine Hand to prepare him for the task to which he was summoned. And so it was with Liang A-fa.

Illustration 2.1: Liang A-fa's old house in Lohstun Village.
Preacher Lei and Colporteur Tsui in doorway

Illustration 2.2: Banyan trees on hill behind Liang A-fa's village home.

Illustration 2.3: The old watch-tower in Liang A-fa's village.

Illustration 2.4 A village school in the Liang A-fa Ancestral Temple.

Notes

1. Percy Ainsworth (1873–1909) published several sermon collections: *The Blessed Life: Short Addresses on the Beatitudes* (1905), *Pilgrim Church and Other Sermons* (1910), *The Silence of Jesus and St. Paul's Hymn to Love* (1910), and *Poems and Sonnets* (1910).

2. Robert Philip, *The Life and Opinions of the Rev. William Milne, D.D., Missionary to China* (Philadelphia: Herman Hooker—Chestnut Street, 1840), 2.

3. Hakka (Mandarin: *kejia* "guest people") and punti (Mandarin *bendi* "local people") are still differentiated today in many contexts.

4. *Fa* appears in a variety of contexts, including words like transmit, publish, emit, and initiate, and is associated with prosperity.

5. The Prophet John in John 1:6 (King James Version).

6. One of the missionary Robert Morrison's first published translations was of the Three Character Classic *Sanzijing.* Morrison's translation appeared in one of his earliest works Robert Morrison, *Horae Sinicae: Translations from the Popular Literature of the Chinese* (London: Black and Parry, 1812).

7. *The Chinese Repository, Vol. IV. From May 1835 to April 1836* [IV:3, July, 1835] (Canton: n.p., 1836), 110.

8. The second major LMS missionary to China, William Milne (1785–1822), did an

early translation of Kangxi's *Sacred Edicts,* and the study of the text was often included in the training of missionaries. William Milne, trans., *The Sacred Edict; Containing Sixteen Maxims of the Emperor Kang-He* (London: Black, Kingsbury, Parbury, and Allen, 1817).

9. From William Wordsworth's poem, "The World is Too Much With Us," in *Poems, in Two Volumes* (1807).

10. Elizabeth A. Morrison, *Memoirs of the Life and Labours of Robert Morrison, D.D,* vol. 1 (London: Longman, Orme, Brown, Green, and Longmans, 1889), 65.

3

Seed Time and Harvest

"Among sinologues and Protestant missionaries Robert Morrison has always stood out in bold relief as their pioneer in China, and his beginnings set the course for all future time, and made the navigation of the China sea of language and society easier for all who came after, whether student or evangelist."

Sir Robert Hart[1]

While Liang A-fa was thus employed, Robert Morrison arrived at Canton about eight o'clock on the evening of September 7, 1807. Because of the fear that the introduction of a missionary might seriously affect trading facilities he, was refused direct passage on British ships, and had to reach China by way of New York. When we recollect that Christianity was proscribed by the Chinese Government, that the Portuguese in Macao opposed any rival to Roman Catholicism, and that all kinds of vexatious restrictions already hindered British trade relations with China we are not very much surprised. But the interesting thing is that in less than eighteen months young Morrison so impressed the business community in Canton and Macao by his character and ability that they felt his expert services as translator and interpreter were necessary for the future success of the East India Company. He was appointed to that position with full knowledge of his missionary purpose, and accepted on the understanding that this would be furthered rather than hindered by such action. And while the Honorable Board in London did occasionally have some anxiety regarding the possible consequences of retaining on their staff an officer who still claimed to be a Protestant missionary, the agents who represented their interests in China found Morrison a wise and efficient servant of the Company. Under the protection of his official position he was able to proceed with his primary task, the translation of the Scriptures. Of this work the Chief of the English factory at Canton wrote to him "I see not why your translating the sacred Scriptures into the Chinese language might not be avowed if occasion called for it. We (members of the Factory) could with reason answer the Chinese thus: 'This volume we deem the best of books. Mr. Morrison happens to be able and willing to render it into your language in order that it may be legible to you. Your approval or disapproval of it rests entirely with yourselves. We conceive he has done a good work.'"[2]

By September of 1810 the translation of the Bible had reached the point where printing might begin. Morrison decided to commence with the Book of Acts, and to print a thousand copies. Before leaving London Morrison had transcribed a Chinese manuscript in the British Museum containing a Harmony of the Gospels, the Acts of the Apostles, and the Pauline epistles. This was the work of some unknown Jesuit priest, and proved of great assistance in translation. It is safe to infer that the task could not have been completed with such rapidity even by such an indefatigable worker if he had not been indebted to this nameless helper. In the translation of a book like the Acts of the Apostles theological and ecclesiastical differences would not interfere with such a partnership. The arrangement for printing was made through Morrison's assistant and tutor Tsae Low-heen, a scholarly man engaged by the missionary soon after his arrival at Canton.[3] Low-heen afterwards confessed he was a party to charging his master between two and three hundred dollars more for this order than the proper price. But it has to be remembered that both assistant and printers ran a very serious risk, as is shown by the following extract from an Imperial edict of that period. It is quoted by Morrison in a letter written on April 2, 1812: "From this time forward such Europeans as shall privately print books and engage preachers to pervert the multitude, and the Manchus and the Chinese who, deputed by Europeans, shall propagate their religion, bestowing names (i.e., baptizing) and disquieting numbers, shall be dealt with as follows: The chief or principal offender shall be summarily executed. Those who spread their religion quietly to a few and without giving names shall be imprisoned awaiting the time of execution. Those who only follow such a religion and are unwilling to recant shall be exiled."[4] No wonder the printers wanted more money. They tried to camouflage their work on Acts by putting a false label on the cover.

In that same year—1810—Liang A-fa's mother died, and he returned to the village home for her funeral. During these years in the city he would be back at least twice in each year, at the Ching Ming festival about Easter time when the family graves are worshipped, and at Chinese New Year, the national holiday. He had now completed his apprenticeship, and part of his wages as a journeyman printer would be remitted for the support of his parents and brother. It is not unlikely that a heavy share of the funeral expenses would fall upon him, and even a poor Chinese family likes to have a presentable funeral. The idolatrous ceremonies common to such an occasion all meant expense. But as she was his mother, and because her son shared her superstitious fears, we may be sure he did not grudge parting with his hard-earned savings that her body might have worthy burial in a propitious plot, and her soul find rest in the Western paradise. There is reason to fear he had not saved a great deal, as he later confessed to wasting his earnings with worthless companions in intemperance and gambling.

Soon after his sad loss and the young block cutter's return to the city his occupation brought him into contact with Robert Morrison. From the human viewpoint the meeting was quite accidental and incidental, but the Christian can see in it God's appointment. The criticism is still heard that Morrison's converts were all drawn from among his own servants. The implication is that their profession was motivated by self-interest. The critics are either ignorant of the actual facts or willfully blind to the truth. It is true the men baptized by Morrison were, or had been, in his employment. For this reason they enjoyed the opportunity of regular Christian instruction in their own language, and were in constant contact with a noble Christian gentleman. The very few that sought baptism did so at grave personal risk, and were only received after long probation and careful teaching. Not only did they place themselves under the ban of the Chinese authorities by their acceptance of the Christian faith, but they were ostracized by relatives and friends. By their choice of the Christian way of living they voluntarily sacrificed such emoluments of their foreign connection as were inconsistent with such a profession. That some of the early converts failed under the test is not strange. But let us be just to the men who denied themselves, and took up their cross, and followed Christ. Some of them will be mentioned in this book. Liang A-fa was not a member of Morrison's household staff. He was a block cutter in a printing establishment in the neighborhood of the foreign factories, and was engaged through Low-heen to engrave the blocks used for printing the New Testament.[5] There is no evidence that he heard the Gospel at first from the lips of the missionary. His earliest contact was through reading the blocks he was employed to engrave.

The man who won Liang A-fa for Christ was William Milne who, with his young wife, arrived from Scotland in 1813 to join Morrison in his missionary labors. They landed at Macao on Sunday July 4, but their coming was so resented by the Portuguese authorities that Milne was given eighteen days in which to leave the colony. He was smuggled into the factory area at Canton, and there secretly began his study of the Chinese language. By the end of the year it was evident to both Morrison and Milne that the time was not yet ripe for definitely establishing a mission in China. Before Morrison left England this eventuality had been foreseen. Writing to his father in 1806 he says "I met the directors (of the L.M.S.) on Tuesday last when it was agreed by the committee that I should proceed by the first conveyance to Madras, thence pass on to Malacca, there leave my luggage and pay a visit to Canton to see whether or not I could settle there. If I can I shall send to Malacca for my books. If not I shall return and take up my residence at Malacca, where there are a few thousands of Chinese, and where I shall endeavor to learn the language."[6] Coming by America this plan was altered, but Morrison was just considering moving to Malacca when he was given the appointment by the East India Company which allowed him to remain in China. The only question now was whether Malacca was the most suitable place to establish the Mission. It was decided Milne should visit the chief centers of Chinese settlement in the East Indies, distributing Scriptures and investigating possibilities for an opening. On Milne's return Malacca, in the strait between Sumatra and the Malay Peninsula, was chosen. The British authorities there were very cordial, and the climate was healthy. The port was easily accessible to other towns in the Archipelago where there were Chinese communities, and was on the direct line of ships passing between India and China. When Mr. and Mrs. Milne sailed for their new station in April 1815 they took with them the printer Liang A-fa, recommended as a capable and faithful workman by Dr. Morrison. A-fa had not only been engaged on the printing of the New Testament. Even in his brief stay at Canton Milne had made such rapid progress in his mastery of Chinese that he was able to write a treatise on the life of Christ. After the style had been corrected by Morrison the blocks were engraved by A-fa, and the book was printed in February 1815.

Liang A-fa has often been wrongly spoken of as the first Protestant convert in China. Even competent authorities such as Dr. S. Wells Williams,

Dr. J. Legge and the Rev. Wm. Gillespie made this mistake. They were naturally followed by later writers. The letters of Morrison and Milne, however,
leave us in no doubt that the first convert was Tsae A-ko, the younger
brother of Low-heen, Morrison's assistant. This young man, then twenty-
one years of age, carne to the missionary's household during his first year
in China. The brothers were the sons of a Chinese ship-owner at Macao.
The family fortune was lost when the ship was wrecked in the China Sea
when returning from Batavia. The father died when A-ko was sixteen. They
had been given a good Chinese education, although A-ko's delicate health
during youth prevented his taking full advantage of his opportunities. Morrison was greatly attracted to him. Less than a year after arrival he wrote
"There is one boy, a fatherless lad, the brother of Low-heen. He possesses
tolerable parts. I wish to pay attention to him."[7] He tried to interest A-ko
in Christ but had not sufficient command of the colloquial to make his
meaning clear. Later the young man was employed by his brother in su-
pervising the printing of the New Testament. Morrison's journal refers to
him in October 1812 under the Mandarin romanization A-fo. By that time
he was a regular attendant at daily prayers and at service on Sundays, and
asked the missionary to teach him how to pray. One day he brought some
idols to show to Morrison, and said he accepted what he had been taught
about the uselessness of worshipping such things. Then he asked for baptism but wished to receive the rite secretly without even letting his brother
know. Morrison was not satisfied with his conduct, however, as he had a
bad temper and quarreled with the brother and other employees, and so he
dismissed him. He does not seem to have cherished resentment, because
although living some miles away he continued to attend the Sunday service.
He formed the habit of prayer, and confessed to the missionary that he had
not fulfilled his duty to his relatives and friends, and that his heart was sinful. After a long period of testing and many evidences of a genuine change
A-ko wrote out a statement of his faith, and Morrison decided to baptize
him. This he did on July 16, 1814, at a spring of water issuing from the foot
of a lofty hill by the seaside at Macao. The water from the same spring still
gurgles down the hillside, being gathered in a drinking fountain at a point
where it is crossed by a public road, and collected in small reservoirs on
the seashore which are now used for washing clothes. Morrison's journal
thus records the event. "At a spring of water issuing from the foot of a lofty
hill by the seaside away from human observation, I baptized, in the Name
of the Father, Son, and Holy Spirit, the person whose name and character

have been given above. Oh, that the Lord may cleanse him from all sin by the blood of Jesus; and purify his heart by the influences of the Holy Spirit! May he be the first-fruits of a great harvest, one of millions who shall come and be saved."[8] Tsae A-ko was not again employed by Morrison. He adhered to his Christian profession until his death from pulmonary consumption in 1819. One of the Protestant Chinese churches in Macao commemorates his name, the baptismal spring still flows down the hill into the ocean, and the prayer of the lonely pioneer is being answered.

Notes

1. Robert Hart (1835–1911), was a British official, born in Northern Ireland, who began his service in China in 1854 and soon rose to become the Inspector General of China's Imperial Maritime Custom Service, a position which he held for decades.

2. Elizabeth A. Morrison, *Memoirs of the Life and Labours of Robert Morrison*, 1:195.

3. The Catholic gospel harmony that Morrison and Yong Sam-Tak copied out is now held by the Hong Kong Bible Society.

4. Elizabeth A. Morrison, *Memoirs of the Life and Labours of Robert Morrison*, 1:336. Morrison wrote "Tartars," where McNeur translates it as "Manchus."

5. Low-heen was the oldest brother of the first convert, mentioned below.

6. Elizabeth A. Morrison, *Memoirs of the Life and Labours of Robert Morrison*, 1:90.

7. Ibid., 226.

8. Ibid., 410.

4

Brighter than the Noonday Sun

"The beginnings of conscious aspiration, of self-knowledge, self-reproach, and self-control, have been for every one of us deeply involved in the acquaintance of good men and women. It was what we saw in them that wakened us."

PROFESSOR H. R. MACKINTOSH, D.D.[1]

Soon after arrival at Malacca Liang A-fa became an earnest seeker after the Truth. Can we trace the influences that led to this change? His previous contact with Morrison, and his acquaintance with Scripture through the blocks he had been engraving, were probably not without some effect on his mind and heart. They would at least provoke questions. Then he had been taken from his old surroundings and worthless companions, and recognized the opportunity for a new beginning. We are very fortunate in having a translation of A-fa's own account of his experience which we quote:

> Before I believed in the Savior, though I knew myself to be a sinner I did not know how to obtain pardon. I used to go every new and full moon to the temple, and prayed to the gods to protect me, but though I worshipped with my body my heart still cherished evil thoughts and desires, together with designs of cheating and lying, which never departed from my mind. After a time I was brought to Malacca in the family of a missionary, who preached to his domestics the doctrine of salvation through Jesus. I attended his ministrations, but my heart was not interested. Sometimes I looked at the Scriptures and heard them explained, but I did not fully comprehend their meaning. Hearing the missionary exhort men not to go and worship the gods, I used to say "This is a strange

kind of doctrine. According to this gilt paper and sacrificial candles, gold flowers and paper money, must be useless and sinful. I fear that Buddha will soon bring punishment and death on such an opponent of the gods, and then we shall see what will happen to his doctrines!"

A few months later a priest of Buddha came from China and lived in the temple of Kwanyin, (the Goddess of Mercy) just near. He visited me frequently, and I asked him how I was to obtain the pardon of sins. He answered "Recite daily the true forms of devotion, and Buddha, who resides in the Western heavens, will remit the sins of your whole family. If a person gives a little money to the priest to chant the prayers for him he will in his next life be born into a rich family, and will not be sent to suffer misery in hell." When I heard this I desired to become a follower of Buddha. The priest immediately sent me a volume of prayers and asked me to repeat, them, saying that if I recited them a thousand times I should cancel all the debts of sin in my former life. I accordingly began to recite the prayers. But one evening while sitting alone it came into my mind that I had committed many real sins, and could hardly expect by reciting prayers, without performing a single virtuous act, to obtain forgiveness.

In the meanwhile I heard the missionary preach the doctrine of atonement through Jesus, and at my leisure I examined the Scriptures, which forbade uncleanness, deceit, and idolatry. Then I thought "These are good books, exhorting men to depart from iniquity. Moreover the doctrines are attested by the miracles of Jesus, therefore the book must certainly be true." I then listened to the expounding of the Scriptures, and on the Sabbath read the Bible more attentively, requesting the missionary to explain it to me. I asked what was meant by Jesus making atonement for sin. The missionary told me that Jesus was the Son of God sent into the world to suffer for the sins of men in order that all who believe in Him might obtain salvation. Feeling myself to be a sinner I asked how I was to obtain pardon. The missionary said "If you believe in Jesus, God will receive you as His adopted son, and in the world to come bestow on you everlasting life." On returning to my room I thought with myself 'I am a great sinner, and if I do not depend on the merits of Christ how can God forgive me?' I then determined to become a disciple of Jesus and requested baptism.[2]

The above is a personal testimony of the greatest possible value. Liang A-fa had come through a genuine religious experience. He had become deeply conscious of moral responsibility and knew himself a sinner. He earnestly sought forgiveness by the traditional and popular way of Buddha's priest, but failed to find satisfaction. There had been awakened in his soul a desire for peace with God, a God who was just and could justify the sinner. He was ready to say with Augustine "Lord Thou hast made us for Thyself, and our hearts are restless till they find rest in Thee." In Jesus Christ as portrayed in Scripture and preached by the missionary he found what he sought—the way to God. While this statement is so simple, clear, and satisfying, we need not infer that it exhausts all the influences that had been working in the printer's heart. He had been employed not only on the Scriptures, but also on the treatise Milne prepared on the life of Christ. It has often happened that where the somewhat disconnected narrative of the Gospels has made little impression on the reader, the ordered story in its historical and geographical setting, with enlightening explanations and apt illustrations, has brought a vision of the reality and worth of the Savior. The unavoidably crude and faulty style of the earliest translation of the New Testament, with its strange names and unfamiliar teaching, made its understanding extremely difficult for its Chinese readers. But Milne's tracts were different. In them there was no need to sacrifice an acceptable diction for an accurate translation, and this story of our Lord's life must have touched the tender conscience, and appealed to the seeking heart of A-fa. The printer read more than the missionary's writings. He saw in him the translation into personality of the Christ life. He was a constant visitor to the mission house. There he was introduced to the first Christian family he had met. The children would appeal to the lonely man, specially the twins born unexpectedly—and thus amidst grave anxiety—four days after sailing from China. At daily family worship, to which all the household servants and workmen gathered, he listened not only to the strange teaching, but to the earnest prayers of this man of God. Milne's biographer records the fact that when he first appeared before the Aberdeen committee of the London Missionary Society its members were afraid this uncouth rustic would not make a suitable missionary to the polite people of China. It was after they heard him pray that their scruples vanished, and they recognized his true worth.

The anniversary of Liang A-fa's baptism might well be remembered as a red letter day in the calendar of the Chinese Church, specially as his birthday is unknown. The occasion so impressed the Rev. Wm. Milne that he left a careful record of the event. In his journal under date Sabbath, November 3, 1816, he wrote:

At twelve o'clock this day I baptized, in the Name of the adorable Trinity, Liang Kung-Fa, commonly called Liang A-fa. The service was performed in a room of the mission house. Care had been taken by previous conversation, instruction, and prayer to prepare him for this sacred ordinance. This had continued for a considerable time. Finding him still steadfast in his wish to become a Christian I baptized him. The change produced in his sentiments and conduct is, I hope, the effect 'of Christian faith and of that alone. Yet who of mortals can know the heart? Several searching questions were proposed to him in private, and an exercise suited to a candidate for baptism composed and given to him to read and meditate upon. He belongs to the province of Kwangtung, is a single man about thirty-three years of age, and has no relatives living except a father and a brother. He can read a plain book with ease, but has had only a common education, and is of a steady character and frugal habits. His temper is not so sociable and engaging as that of many other Chinese. He was formerly stiff and obstinate and occasionally troublesome, but of late there has hardly been anything of this kind to complain of .... He wished to be baptized exactly at twelve o'clock, when, to use his own words, 'the shadow inclines neither one way nor the other.' What his view was in fixing upon this precise time I cannot tell, but I suppose it arose from the remains of that superstitious regard to 'times' which prevails so generally among the Chinese.[3] I told him God had not distinguished one hour from another, and that he, as a disciple of Christ, must regard every day and hour alike, except the Sabbath, which is devoted specially to the service of God. Aware that some superstitious attachments may, for a considerable time, hang about the first converts from paganism, and that it is in the church, and under the ordinances thereof, that these attachments are to be entirely destroyed, I did not think it advisable to delay administering the initiatory ordinance.[4]

By such an attitude the missionary of over a century ago manifested both his charity and his wisdom. It may possibly have been the exact time of his first birth, of which the Chinese keep careful record because of its supposed influence on the subsequent events of life, that led A-fa to choose this hour for the solemn rite which was to mark his birth from above. It might conceivably be because this man felt there was a special fitness in beginning at midday. St. Paul's conversion may have been in his mind. "Every good gift and every perfect present is from heaven, and comes down from the Father of the heavenly lights, about whom there is no variation of changing shadow. Of his own accord He brought us into being through the message of truth, so that we might be a kind of firstfruits among His creatures." Jas. 1:17–18 (Goodspeed).[5] Whatever the reason it was wisdom on the part of the missionary to acquiesce in such a harmless request. Hurt may be done by the bringing of too narrow a standard to the task of admitting converts into the church. Insistence by Western pastors on an experience identical with that familiar in their own lands will create hindrances where our Lord would find none. Milne was very careful that the candidate clearly understood the step he was taking. For some time before the ordinance he met with A-fa once a week for special preparation. On these occasions passages of Scripture which had troubled A-fa in his private reading were explained. But the missionary did not wait for the knowledge of riper Christian experience before administering baptism.

The following are the questions Milne put to the candidate and his answers thereto:

Q. "Have you truly turned from idols to serve the living and true God, the Creator of heaven and earth?"

A. "This is my heart's desire."

Q. "Do you know and feel that you are a sinful creature and unable to save yourself?"

A. "I know it."

Q. "Do you really believe that Jesus Christ is Son of God and Savior of the world, and do you trust in Him alone for salvation?"

A. "This is my heart's desire."

Q. "Do you expect any worldly advantage, profit, or gain by your becoming a Christian?"

A. "None, I receive baptism because it is my duty."

Q. "Do you resolve from this day till the day of your death to live in obedience to all the commandments and ordinances of God, and in justice and righteousness before men?"

A. "This is my determination, but I fear my strength is not equal to it."[6]

Both questions and answers are self-revealing. It would be difficult to frame five brief questions more basic and inclusive. Milne adds to his record the words "On my part the ordinance was dispensed with mingled affection, joy, hope, and fear. May he be made faithful unto death, and as he is the firstfruits of this branch of the mission, may an abundant harvest follow, to the joy of the Church and the honor of Christ."[7]

For three years after his baptism A-fa continued to work with Milne but "no longer a servant, but more than a servant, a brother beloved."[8] He progressed steadily in Christian knowledge, and proved a most diligent student. Not that he invariably satisfied his teacher. That would be too much to expect from a Scottish theologian and a Chinese convert. The missionary writes "I had given A-fa John 3:16 to write a little on as a little trial. He wrote very good sense but left out the article of redemption, and, excepting the divinity of Christ, made it exactly a Socinian discourse on the design of Christ: coming into the world."[9] Milne's conclusion to this incident was a criticism of the teacher rather than of the pupil: "Things delivered in the general are apt to lose their effect."[10] Knowing something of A-fa's ethical and religious heritage we are not surprised at his difficulties. It is one thing for a Chinese Christian to repeat the articles of the creed which he has been taught by the missionary; it is quite another for him to honestly use his own mind in the explanation of a passage from Scripture.

A-fa had now a new interest in everything that pertained to the work of the mission. A printing press and founts of Malay and English type had been procured, and the printers were taught to set up in English and Malay and to use the press, while still continuing the printing of the Chinese Bible and tracts from blocks. The restrictions under which Morrison was laboring in Macao and Canton made it increasingly evident that most of the printing and publishing would have to be done at Malacca.

On November 10, 1818, another part of Morrison's long-cherished plans began to take concrete form when the foundation stone of the Anglo-Chinese College was laid at Malacca. Years before (1813) Morrison wrote "I wish we had an institution at Malacca for the training of missionaries, European and native, and designed for all the countries beyond the Ganges. There also let there be that powerful engine the Press. The first triumphs of the Gospel will, I think, be by means of native missionaries and the Bible."[11] He hoped this institution would facilitate an amicable literary intercourse betwixt England and the nations in which the Chinese written language was employed.

Students attending were not to be required to profess Christianity nor obliged to attend Christian worship, although all would be invited to do so. Morrison gave £1000 towards the erection of the building and £100 per annum for its current expenses, besides a very valuable gift of books for its library. Milne was the first principal. Suspicion of the new venture was so strong that when a primary school was opened a small weekly sum of money had to be offered to each child before parents would send them. However the school soon overcame its initial difficulties. Liang A-fa was naturally interested in this scheme and later was considered, although somewhat irregular, a theological student in connection with the College.

Milne had commenced the publication of a monthly magazine in Chinese, and to this Liang A-fa became a frequent contributor. Thus he began a new phase of his training which was to fit him for the task of proclaiming by written and spoken words his experience of salvation in Christ.

Notes

1. Hugh Ross Mackintosh (1870–1936) was a professor of theology at New College, Edinburgh.

2. William H. Medhurst, *China: Its State and Prospects with Especial Reference to the Spread of the Gospel; Containing Allusions to the Antiquity, Extent, Population, Civilization, Literature, and Religion of the Chinese* (Boston: Crocker & Brewster, 1838), 250–251.

3. The Daoist scholar Michael Saso suggested possibilities for the noontime baptism (personal communication). He notes that noon is pure yang and water is pure yin, so the two together are pure Qi ("energy," "power," or "life force"). Secret societies, popular in the diaspora, may also have been a model. Saso also allowed that biblical accounts may have been suggestive of a late-morning or midday account. While the missionaries do not suggest such a possibility, McNeur (below) offers an interpretation based on James 1:17.

4. William Milne, *A Retrospect of the First Ten Years of the Protestant Mission to China* (Malacca: Anglo-Chinese Press, 1820), 177–78. This account was widely reproduced, but I believe it first appeared in Robert Morrison, "Baptism of a Chinese," *Evangelical Magazine* (Oct. 1815), 426.

5. The "Goodspeed" here refers to the Bible translation made by Edwin Goodspeed and J. M. Powis Smith. The New Testament was published in 1923, the Old Testament in 1927, and the complete Bible in 1931, all by the University of Chicago Press.

6. William Milne, *A Retrospect of the First Ten Years of the Protestant Mission to China*, 179.

7. Ibid.

8. Robert Philip, *The Life and Opinions of the Rev. William Milne*, 208.

9. Ibid., 266.

10. Ibid.

11. Elizabeth A. Morrison, *Memoirs of the Life and Labours of Robert Morrison*, 1:355.

5

The Cost of a Bride

"I know that your heart and Christ are married together. It were not good to make a divorce. Rue not of that meeting and marriage with such a Husband. Pray for me, His prisoner."[1]

Letters of Samuel Rutherford.

A Chinese abroad is seldom completely happy, and Liang. A-fa's heart yearned for his own kindred, from whom he had been so long separated. The clan system draws its own sons together however far they may have roamed. In a pine-grove outside a great village to the North of Canton, from which thousands of men have gone to other lands, there is a wayside shelter inscribed with words "The place to which the scattered flock returns." Its villagers have wandered to the ends of the earth, but their hearts are still in the ancestral home, and their deepest longing is to get back to its shelter. If death should rob them of that dear privilege their one comfort is in the hope that their dust will be laid to rest in the family tomb. In the Straits Settlements and the Hands of the East Indies, including the Philippine Islands, the Chinese emigrants have found so congenial a climate and such pleasant conditions that they have taken their families with them and made their permanent home there. But Liang A-fa was alone. His loneliness was made more acute by the loss in the beginning of 1819 of a true friend. This was Mrs. Milne, who had taught him what a Christian home could be. Her death was a sore bereavement to her devoted husband, and his journal afterwards was often blotted and blurred by his tears as he thought of her. Perhaps it was the sorrow in the mission house that led A-fa to think so anxiously of his own folk, and the recollection of its former joy that finally decided him to seek a life partner of his own. At any rate he left Malacca soon afterwards for Canton. Mr. Milne wrote in his journal "A-fa, the Chinese Christian, left us. After giving him some suitable instruction, after prayers and many tears, we parted. The Lord keep him steady and faithful unto death."[2]

When he saw again the trees on the hilltop, the old watchtower rising by its side, and the ancestral temple in front of his native village, and trod the familiar path along the top of the flood-dykes, the greatest change the years had brought was in himself. He came back with big plans for the future. He had brought his savings with which to arrange the wedding, and build a new house for his father. But he had hardly entered the village before discovering it was a different matter being a Christian there from following Christ in a mission compound at Malacca. Many a Chinese emigrant who has accepted Christianity abroad has compromised and fallen when faced with the situation which met him on return home. It is impossible for people of the West, with their individualistic life, to appreciate the severity of the test. In the case of A-fa it was more trying because, in an important sense, it was without precedent. Had he become a Mohammedan he would at least have found a thriving community of fellow-believers in Canton. If he had joined the Roman Catholic Church he would have received a welcome in one of the numerous congregations throughout the province. But he was alone. He was the solitary representative of the outlawed Protestant religion. Not only was he expected to take part in certain ancestral and idolatrous rites on his reunion with the family, but he would be quite unable to prevent the many pagan practices common to Chinese weddings. What did he do? There was no possibility of a quiet ceremony arranged to suit the queer notions of the man whose sojourn abroad had so strangely affected him. The bride's family would never accept such a shameful departure from tradition. A wedding for a returned emigrant would be a clan function. We can only imagine how grieved the father and relatives must have been when the usual felicitations, feastings, and rejoicings were marred by the obstinate scruples of the bridegroom. The writer knows a Chinese Christian who, even in this century, was seized by relatives at his wedding, and in spite of his protests and resistance was forced into the attitude of worship before the ancestral tablets and the idol shrine. We are not told what A-fa did, nor what was done to him. But we do know that what happened decided him to make it clear once and for all to his fellow-villagers that he was a Christian, and made him earnestly desirous they should be awakened to the evils of idolatry.

The way by which he could best bear this witness was indicated by the methods of Morrison and Milne and his own handicraft. He took his Chinese Bible, not yet quite complete, and prepared a tract which embodied a few of the clearest and most important portions of Scripture dealing with God as Creator, the sin of idolatry, and the need of repentance and faith in Christ. It contained the ten commandments and three hymns and, prayers. This he entitled "A brief explanatory abstract of the plan of world salvation." There were only thirty-seven pages, but it was the first tract composed and printed by a Chinese Christian. He took the manuscript to Canton and showed it to Morrison. Having received his hearty approval he had the blocks engraved, and printed two hundred copies which he intended taking back to the country and circulating among his fellow-villagers. Unexpectedly the police seized him, with the blocks and books, before he could leave the city, and brought him before the magistrate. Perhaps some workman had given the information which led to his arrest. Another man, a former servant of Milne, was arrested with him, and they were forced to tell under threat of torture all they knew regarding Morrison and Milne, and to give the names of the Chinese employed by the former. In consequence the police were sent to Morrison's room in the East India Company's factory to arrest Tsae A-sam, the younger brother of Tsae A-ko. Morrison concealed him locked up in his own bedroom.

A-fa pleaded before the magistrate that there was nothing harmful in his little book, but on the contrary it exhorted men to virtue. The judge replied "Your book is stuff and nonsense, and I punish you for going abroad. Flog him!" At that time Chinese law regarding emigration was stated in the following terms: "All officers of government, soldiers, and private citizens who clandestinely proceed to sea for trade, or who remove to foreign islands for the purpose of inhabiting and cultivating the same, shall be punished according to the law against communicating with rebels and enemies, and consequently suffer death by being beheaded."[3] This law continued on the statute book until 1860. Although it was never rigidly enforced it could be used by local officials to extort money from returned emigrants or their families.

A-fa's books and blocks were destroyed, and he was cruelly beaten on the soles of his feet until the blood ran down his legs.[4] Thrown into prison after this punishment he reflected on the strange outcome of his plans for spreading the Gospel among his kinsmen. Convinced he had done right in printing his book he felt it must be for his sins that he suffered. So he confessed and sought God's pardon. He was released temporarily in order that he might seek money to pay a heavy fine. For this he sought Morrison's help, but the missionary felt it would be a dangerous precedent to accede to such a request. It must have been a sore experience for both. Mr. Morrison writes "He was a fellow-Christian and suffered for the sake of Jesus. What was I to do? Had I given him the money it would have been reported that a servant of the East India Company had given him one thousand dollars (for it would have been exaggerated) and the proceeding would have operated as a precedent for similar attacks, and for frauds (under pretence of suffering) being practiced upon me by persons I may employ in the concerns of the mission. I therefore refused." Mr. Morrison, however, persuaded influential Chinese to help in securing his final release. The money with which he had planned to build the new house for his father and the young bride had to be paid to the magistrate. Even his clothes were taken from him by the police. He was also forbidden residence in the city of Canton. Morrison wrote to the Society "I am happy that this Chinese Christian does not suffer as an evildoer, but for Christ's sake, and neither he nor we have reason to be ashamed. It is not impossible but that this land must be watered with the blood of many martyrs before the Gospel prevails generally." Liang A-fa summed up the result of this experience for himself in the words "I did not dare to turn my back on the Lord Jesus."

On his banishment from Canton he returned to his village home, and after forty days with his family set out again for Malacca. There he spent another busy year in work and study with Mr. Milne. The translation and printing of the whole Bible had now been completed. Of the Old Testament the books from Deuteronomy to Job were the work of Milne, the rest had been done by Morrison. To honor Milne's share in the great task Glasgow University conferred on him the degree of Doctor of Divinity. The same institution had bestowed a similar honor on Morrison the previous year. We can imagine the joy A-fa would have in the possession of the whole Bible in his own language. Morrison connects his subsequent return to China with the completion of this work, implying that the Christian printer felt that he had no longer sufficient justification for residence abroad. Now that God's Providence and the devotion of his missionary friends had given his people the Bible, it must be his task to carry its message to them. Milne, in writing to Morrison on November 3, 1820, says "Should A-fa continue steadfast in his profession, and in the pursuit of knowledge, and in his desire for usefulness for a year or two longer, would it be advisable to ordain him before his return to China, that he might be qualified to administer Christian ordinances in case of your death, or in case of any convert being obtained who could not come to you for baptism? He talks of returning next summer, but I hope he may be persuaded to remain a little longer. Do take this into serious consideration. What a mercy and comfort would it be for us to be able to send from our little College, in course of two or three years from its commencement, a native preacher tolerably fitted for the blessed work of preaching the Gospel! I wish what we do to be as it were a joint act. Tell me your whole mind."[5]

A-fa could not be persuaded to stay longer at Malacca. One very good reason was that a little son had been born in the home at Lohtsun whom he very much wanted to see. And his experience of a united Christian home in the mission house, and the influence of a Christian wife and mother, had awakened in his heart a great longing to win his wife for Christ. So he came back again to the old home, rejoicing this time in his boy—the choicest gift a Chinese can receive. He read and explained the Scripture to his wife, prayed for her and with her, and soon had the added joy of hearing her confess faith in his Savior. She was the first woman in China to make such a profession as a fruit of Protestant effort. But how was she to receive the ordinance of initiation to the visible Church which had been so precious an experience to himself? The long journey to Canton or Macao with the little child seemed impossible. Should the ceremony be delayed? We may be sure the decision was not hastily reached, but finally A-fa determined to baptize her himself. So there in that plain room of the cottage home, with water drawn from the village well, and using a rice-bowl as a baptismal font, this man received into the Christian fellowship his first trophy for Christ.[6] The service conducted by the missionary at his own baptism would be the model followed. We are sure there was reading of appropriate Scripture and direct earnest prayer. A hymn of praise may have been chanted, because A-fa was familiar with the place of song in worship. As this ignorant young Chinese woman, the babe strapped on her back, took the vow to turn from idol to Christ, and her workman husband sprinkled the water of the holy sacrament upon her bowed head, no magnificent cathedral could have been more really the house of God. A-fa, recalling that hallowed hour some years later, said "From that time we have been of one heart and one mind in worshipping and serving the one only living and true God, the Ruler and Governor of the universe, and in endeavoring to turn those around us from the service of dumb idols."[7] The wife, whose surname was Lai, came from another ward of the same village, so that the couple would have many common interests.

God's goodness to him in the conversion of his wife strengthened Liang A-fa's resolve to give his life for the preaching of the Gospel. He was conscious that he needed further preparation. Husband and wife discussed the matter together, and she consented to his going back to Malacca for continued study under Dr. Milne. So in 1821 this first Protestant Chinese couple parted for the Gospel's sake, and the wife with her little son were left behind in the village home. What testing her new faith must have suffered we can only guess. Unable to read, knowing only the bare rudiments of Christian truth, alone in the heathen community in which she had been brought up, hers was the harder part.

A-fa was welcomed as a brother by Dr. Milne, and it was arranged that he should give most of his time to the study of the Bible. But it was sadly evident to the student that his beloved teacher was far from well. He was suffering under the heavy strain of the many responsibilities he was carrying, made doubly heavy by his constant sorrow over the death of his wife. He had frequent hemorrhages of the lungs. A voyage was taken to Penang, but this change of scene and climate brought no improvement, and he returned to die at his post on June 2, 1822. He was only thirty-seven years of age—about the same age as A-fa. Of an ardent, impetuous, and determined mind, and being fully assured he was in the mission field in response to a Divine call, he was accustomed to say "When I am convinced a thing is right I could go through the fire to accomplish it." His work in translating the Scriptures and as Principal of the Anglo-Chinese College has already been mentioned. He also edited a Chinese monthly and an English quarterly magazine.[8] He translated and composed a number of booklets and tracts. One of the best known was "The Conversation between Two Friends"—perhaps the most fruitful Chinese tract ever written. The pen name he used for all his Chinese publications was "The Catholic Lover."[9] He left a wonderful record of unremitting toil, saintliness of life, and high attainment, but the greatest work Dr. Milne had done in the nine brief years of his devoted missionary career was the winning and training of his Chinese brother Liang A-fa.

Illustration 5.1: Rev. Wm. Milne, D.D.

Illustration 5.2: From a Chinese Painting of the English Factories
at Canton as they were in Dr. Morrison's Time

Notes

1. Samuel Rutherford was a famous Puritan author (1600-1661). This is from his letter, "To Mrs. Stuart, wife of the Provost of Aye," written in Aberdeen, 1637.

2. Robert Philip, *The Life and Opinions of the Rev. William Milne, D.D.*, 301–2.

3. According to several recent sources which contain this same English quote, this comes from the *Da Qing Luli* (Imperial laws of the Great Qing), Section 225 (1712). The sources they cite are later than McNeur, and I have not been able to identify the original source of the English quotation, which is often reproduced word for word.

4. This description appears in Liang's own Chinese description of his suffering (see the section "Liang as Confessor" in the editor's critical introduction to this volume). See also Philip, *The Life and Opinions of the Rev. William Milne*, 210.

5. Elizabeth A. Morrison, *Memoirs of the Life and Labours of Robert Morrison*, 2:74–75.

6. Liang himself in the Chinese account does not distinguish it as a rice bowl, but presumably most bowls in China can be described as rice bowls.

7. "Brief Memoir of the Evangelist, Leang Afa," *The Missionary Herald* 30:10 (October 1834), 357.

8. These were *The Indo-Chinese Gleaner* (published 1817–1822 in three volumes in English) and *The Chinese Monthly* (*Cha shisu meiyue tongji zhuan*, published 1815–1821 in seven volumes in Chinese).

9. Milne's pen name was Boaizhe. The tract *Two Friends* went on to become quite famous, and Harvard Professor of Chinese Patrick Hanan writes that this work "was probably the most frequently reprinted Chinese novel *of any kind* during the [nineteenth] century," Patrick Hanan, *Chinese Fiction of the Nineteenth and Early Twentieth Centuries: Essays* (Masters of Chinese Studies 2; New York: Columbia University Press, 2004), 60. On this work, see also Daniel Bays, "The Two Friends," in Barnett and Fairbank, *Christianity in China: Early Protestant Writings* (Harvard Studies in American–East Asian Relations 9; Cambridge: Committee on American–East Asian Relations, distributed by Harvard University Press, 1985).

6

The Chinese Gospel

"The peoples of the Far East have their own spiritual and religious inheritance, which is in some aspects different from that of the western nations. Their inheritance helps them to understand the purpose of God in Jesus Christ in their own way."[1]

Dr. Timothy T. Lew

When his friends and teachers died, A-fa felt there was no need of his remaining longer in Malacca. This Chinese Elisha had caught the spirit of the Scottish Elijah, and was eager to carry the message to his own people. Morrison wrote of Milne "A more zealous evangelist never existed," and the same fire had been kindled in A-fa's heart. He returned to his family in China and rejoiced to find them well. We are not surprised to learn that he began his campaign by seeking to win his father, but the old man was unwilling to forsake the faith of his fathers. A-fa went to visit Dr. Morrison at Canton and arranged to bring his little son to his rooms for baptism, and also for vaccination. It is interesting to find this double purpose recorded so long ago. Vaccination for smallpox had been introduced by Dr. Pearson of the East India Company early in the century. In 1933 it is still unusual to find anyone using modern methods of vaccination in A-fa's home district. A scab is taken from a smallpox patient and is used to provoke an attack in children, so that they may be immune in later life. It should be said, however, that in other parts of the province scientific methods of inoculation are widely used and frequently free of cost.

Dr. Morrison was much impressed by A-fa's visit and records "Liang A-fa, after reading II Chron. 7:12–22, knelt with the missionary who writes this and prayed in Chinese, a prayer dictated by the circumstances and feelings of the moment, with great freedom and fervor. "Blessed be God! O, may the seed sown take root and grow up in China, though man cannot tell how. Lord of the harvest! do Thou water the seed of the Word with showers of the Holy Spirit's influence from heaven." The passage read, which contained God's revelation to Solomon in response to his prayers and sacrifices at the dedication of the temple, with its references to father, son, and subsequent generations, and its comparisons of the blessings of obedience to God with the penalties of idol worship, was eminently appropriate.

On Nov. 20, 1823 he brought his little son, as arranged, to Dr. Morrison for baptism. The name given to a son in China, as already noted, expresses a hope and a prayer. The name this couple had chosen for their boy—Tsen-teh² (Advancing Virtue)—shows their chief desire that he might grow in grace. He was familiarly known afterwards as A-teh, but, like other Chinese of position, he had a number of names used at different times. This practice is rather confusing to the historian. Morrison's journal has this entry: "Today Liang A-fa, our Chinese fellow-disciple, brought his son Liang Tsen-teh, and had him baptized in the name of God the Father, Son and Spirit. Oh! that this small Christian family may be the means of spreading the truth around them in this pagan land."³

A-fa was anxious to continue his theological studies under Dr. Morrison. He felt specially the lack of helps in the way of commentaries in Chinese on the more difficult parts of Scripture, such as the prophets of the Old Testament, and missed the expert guidance Dr. Milne had given him. But, unfortunately for his desire, Dr. Morrison had to leave for England in December of that year. The pioneer had now been on the field for sixteen years without a furlough. Three years previously his wife had died, and his little boy and girl were already in England. He expected the visit to be brief, intending to return within twelve months. His deepest regret was that he was leaving the field without a missionary to care for the work begun by him in Macao and Canton. Appeals to the churches in Britain and America had so far been fruitless. Under such circumstances it was an unspeakable comfort to have Liang A-fa, whom Milne had already so warmly commended for this task, return to China. "To ensure the continuance of Christian ordinances among the few who had renounced idolatry, after a serious consideration of the subject, he dedicated Liang A-fa who had for eight years given evidence of his qualifications for the work, to the office of evangelist among his fellow-countrymen."[4] In the words of A-fa himself "Dr. Morrison laid hands on me, and ordained me to publish to men everywhere the true Gospel."[5] It is quite evident from subsequent statements by missionaries associated with the evangelist that Dr. Morrison's action was accepted as involving full ordination to the Christian ministry. To any objection, whether in the case of the wife's baptism or his own ordination, a statement by Dr. J. A. Hutton, editor of the British Weekly, may be borrowed in reply. "For myself I have never asked for any authority on any proposal, either in the region of faith or in the region of practice, than that, in a sober view of all the circumstances, it had become necessary." From the date of his ordination until his death A-fa's salary was paid by the London Missionary Society.

Dr. Morrison was absent from China much longer than he expected. It was September 19, 1826—nearly three years later—before he landed again in Macao, bringing with him his second wife. There is almost no record of A-fa's work during this long period. Without postal facilities, lacking a knowledge of English, and in the absence of any English friends on the field, it would be impossible for him to send reports to the Society. The story of how he had used his talents was told to Dr. Morrison the day after his arrival. The joy of this reunion was so great that Morrison's disappointment in finding his house and furniture much deteriorated through lack of care, and his valuable library ruined by termites, was forgotten, and he thanked God and took courage. In prayer they gave praise to God together for His kind preservation of their lives and that He had kept them looking to Jesus. The following Sunday Morrison began again his regular services for the Chinese. At the close A-fa presented him with a small volume in Chinese containing explanatory notes on the epistle to the Hebrews, which he had written during the missionary's absence. Morrison says of it: "It is designed to communicate to pagans those views of religion which he derived from the late lamented Milne. I have read a part of it, and considering the few advantages A-fa has had, the work evinces that he has made the Bible his study, although some parts of the composition receive a shade of color in the phraseology from his recent paganism. He wrote also a small essay in favor of the Christian religion which he entitled 'The True Principles of the World's Salvation.'"[6]

The "shade of color" seemingly deprecated by the missionary in this and other cases may not have been altogether a bad thing. In fact it may have been a bit of the "local color" which leading Chinese Christians are now insisting should be the natural mark of an acclimatized Christianity. It would be surprising indeed if a Chinese evangelist did not seek to mediate his message through the phraseology and psychology which represented the religious life of the Chinese people. Only thus could it be popularly understood. Doubtless there was an element of risk. There always has been where the heralds of the Cross have advanced into new territory. The danger is graphically illustrated in the combination of the cross, the cloud and the lotus, representing the fusion of Christianity, Taoism and Buddhism, on the Nestorian tablet at Sianfu in North China.[7]

Dr. Morrison was quite satisfied A-fa had been most faithful and diligent in discharging the duties of his office during the three years. He received from him a brief written account of several conversations with his countrymen on the subject of religion. The following is an example. While travelling on a passage boat A-fa was reading the Gospel of Mark when a fellow-passenger, looking over his shoulder, noticed the expression "till the Son of Man be risen from the dead" and asked what it meant. A-fa told him of the death and resurrection of Jesus to make atonement for sin, confessed his own faith, and preached the Gospel to him. Hearing of the miracles of Jesus the man asked if he had seen them. A-fa answered he had not, but that they were related in the Holy Scriptures. "Have you never read" replied the man, "what Mencius said: 'It would be better to be without books at all than to believe every book'? Although the Western peoples believe these writings it is not necessary for us to credit them." A-fa told him he believed the things recorded in the Bible because he felt himself a sinner, and knew that without a Savior he could not escape punishment. Then, also quoting Mencius, A-fa said "A good man may be deceived by a distorted representation of facts, but cannot be deluded into believing things palpably absurd." Here again we have a bit of the "local color," this time from the ancient classics. A-fa's quotation has an amusing context which was of course familiar to his hearer, and needs to be known in order to appreciate its force. Someone once presented the Prime Minister of Ch'ing with a live fish. He ordered a servant to free it in the pond. The servant cooked and ate it, and afterwards told his master he had obeyed his command, describing how the fish when placed in the water had at first seemed uncertain what to do, and then gradually it appeared to be at home, and finally it swam off in great glee. The master exclaimed, "Back to its element back to its element! "The servant went out and said to his friends "Who said the Prime

Minister was a wise man? I cooked and ate his fish and he cries 'Back to its element!'" Mencius commented on the incident in the words quoted by A-fa. The meaning of the reference is that the good man cannot be fooled into believing anything quite unreasonable, and that the acceptance of the Scriptures by good men proves their credibility.

In reporting A-fa's work during his absence Morrison wrote "In a land like this, full of idols and crowded with idolaters, where persecution is carried on from the throne to the cottage against the disciples of Jesus, we must not be surprised if many resemble Nicodemus, or be what the church historian Milner has called 'pagan Christians'—that is Christians of imperfect knowledge and a timid, or rather, concealed profession. However there is one, whatever the opinion of my brethren may be, who is a decided Christian, and who makes an open confession of his faith. It is Liang A-fa. Indeed, I apprehend that his zeal may exceed his prudence."[8] Soon after Dr. Morrison's return A-fa wrote what is probably his first letter to the London Missionary Society. It was translated and forwarded by Morrison and is quoted in full as a typical example of the evangelist's epistles.

"From Liang A-fa, the first fruits of China to Christ, to British Christians of the London Missionary Society.

"All of us who sincerely believe in our Lord Jesus although dwelling in different places, and not having hitherto seen or known each other, still possess a heart as if we had seen and known each other, for our principles are one, our hearts are one, and our thoughts and hopes are one. Therefore I, Liang A-fa, unite with the venerable teachers and all those who believe in our Lord Jesus Christ, although heretofore we have never seen nor known each other, still there and here our hearts are the same.

"Thinking thus I send a letter of salutation to all in the noble English nation who sincerely believe in our Lord Jesus, both teachers and people. Peace be with you! Peace be with you!

"Now, when God the Most High Ruler wills to convert an individual, to convert a family, or to convert a nation He, by His own inscrutable purpose, causes men to go forth and preach the Gospel to them, and causes men to believe and obey it. Hence I, Liang A-fa, obtained a knowledge of the Gospel's true principles, believing and Obeying our Lord Jesus Christ, along with my whole family. This was from God the most high Ruler's self-induced purpose in causing the venerable teachers Morrison and Milne to come to China to promulgate and explain the true principles of the Gospel, and so enticing me, Liang A-fa, to hear, to believe and to obey them.

"Thus in the tenth chapter of Romans and verse fourteen it is said 'How then shall they call on Him in whom they have not believed, and how shall they believe in Him of whom they have not heard, and how shall they hear without a preacher?'

"As in all the nations of the world there are many doctrines but none can be compared with the principles of the Gospel, I do not now desire to bustle and strive for the things of this, life, but I voluntarily desire to be a learner at the missionary's door, to learn clearly true principles and to promulgate them in my native country. Thus these may cause men to know the Gospel, to believe and obey it, and so I should hope to convert my Chinese countrymen that they may cast away their molten images, and honor and reverence the Lord of heaven, earth, and all things as God.

"But we Chinese, high and low, men of all ranks, are stupefied and deceived and moreover extremely proud and haughty. Besides, the Gospel's true principles are things recently listened to and heard, and the customs of the literati in communicating instruction are different from that of other nations. Therefore I fear that with shallow abilities and meager virtues I shall not be able to teach them. I can only exert to the utmost the strength of a willing mind, and implore God the most high Ruler to confer the Holy Spirit's influence to convert men's hearts.

"But perhaps there may not be ability to effect any great reformation or change. Still, although in the age in which we live we may not see the results, yet we may leave that on record which will transmit the true principles of the Gospel to others, in the hope of converting men of succeeding generations.

"Therefore I earnestly beseech all the venerable teachers and sincere believers in our Lord—those who have virtuous power to employ their virtuous power, those who have talents to employ their talents, and put forth extensively the energies of a heart of benevolence and love to scatter widely the true principles of the Gospel among all nations so that men may be converted. Thus we will not criminally turn our backs on the grace of the most high Lord manifested in the work of human redemption, but, contrariwise, we may perform our duty to the utmost so that in the coming life we may hope our Lord will graciously confer on us the gift of everlasting blessedness in Heaven, where we shall enjoy repose and delight.

"I desire that the peace of our Lord Jesus Christ may be with you to all eternity. Amen."[9]

Notes

1. Also known as Liu Tingfang (1891–1947). This is a quote from Liu's presentation at the First World Conference on Faith and Order held in Lausanne in 1927. For more on Liu see Donald E. MacInnis, "Liu, Timothy Ting-Fang (Lew, T.T.)," 405, in Gerald Anderson, ed., *Biographical Dictionary of Christian Missions* (Grand Rapids: Eerdmans, 1999).

2. Pinyin: *Jinde*.

3. Elizabeth A. Morrison, *Memoirs of the Life and Labours of Robert Morrison*, 2:225.

4. Ibid., 235.

5. Robert Philip, *The Life and Opinions of the Rev. William Milne, D.D.*, 212.

6. Elizabeth A. Morrison, *Memoirs of the Life and Labours of Robert Morrison*, 2:357.

7. This is the famous tablet of the Church of the East, which can still be seen today in Xi'an.

8. Elizabeth A. Morrison, *Memoirs of the Life and Labours of Robert Morrison*, 2:359.

9. "London Missionary Society, Letter from the Native Convert, Leangafa, to the Directors," *Missionary Register* (Dec. 1827) 595–96. McNeur appears to have added the opening appellation to this letter and also made some small stylistic changes.

7

Humanized Literature

"Gairdner believed (for was he not mightily battered with anti-Christian arguments) that there must needs be an apologetic literature, unafraid of controversial points. Silence, he felt, was tantamount to denial of the truth he knew and lived. But the literature must be humanized and written for fellow-men, not only for the defeat of argufiers."[1]

— "Temple Gairdner of Cairo"

The whole foreign community in these pre-treaty days was required by the Chinese Government to vacate the factory area at Canton for several months during the summer of each year. This was doubtless intended to impress on the visitors the temporary nature of their tenure. It was a privilege granted to them by the Manchu lords of the Middle Kingdom year by year. The law which forbade any foreign woman coming to Canton had the same intention. The enforced change allowed Dr. Morrison to spend some time at Macao with his family. It also gave him the necessary leisure to continue Liang A-fa's instruction in theology. In September, 1827, he writes "Liang A-fa has been with me all the summer. He has read a great part of the Scriptures and came to me daily to have explained those parts which he found difficult. When he retired he wrote notes of what he heard. Prayer is that in which A-fa excels. The evidence of his piety is most satisfactory when on his knees. His natural temper is irritable and hasty, and his address is unengaging to his countrymen. As he openly avows his Christianity the pagan domestics vilify and insult him as a renegade from the religion of his fathers and a traitor to his country. A-fa has completed a paraphristic version of the epistle of Paul to the Romans which is useful to us as foreign missionaries by suggesting words and phrases, and enabling us to judge of the correctness of the written views so that we may correct them when wrong."

On the same day A-fa wrote another letter to the Society. This Chinese document, still enclosed in its original envelope, is preserved in its archives in London. It is too long to quote *in toto*, but one paragraph reads:

"If the good people of your country have this virtuous love of others, how could we belong to the Lord and not love the people of our own country. Because of this I am now studying the doctrine with the venerable Dr. Morrison, and have been thus engaged for over a year. I am fortunate in having Dr. Morrison to guide me step by step, and to open my understanding that I may comprehend something of the meaning of the Gospel. The Truth seems to me without limit, and the more one thinks of it the deeper it becomes. I have the desire to complete my studies, but lack the ability. Therefore, day and night, morning and evening, I pray the Lord to give the virtue of His Holy Spirit that He may open my heart and lead me to exert all my ability, so that I may perhaps learn the beginnings, and thus be enabled to repress my lusts and diminish my transgressions. Thus, having rectified my own conduct, I may be able to teach and admonish others. The mere learning of the Truth may appear easy, but to consistently live according to the Truth is very difficult."[2]

When A-fa left his teacher after this long term of study together he was so much moved that he wept, lamenting his failure in converting souls to Christ. He stated his intention of writing short tracts and distributing them as the most practical method of evangelism. Soon after return to his country home he had an encouraging experience which showed him there were those among his countrymen ready to receive the Gospel. A young school teacher named Kwu Tin-ching became so interested that A-fa arranged to live with him for a time in order that they might study Christianity together. One Sunday in January 1828 this new convert was baptized by A-fa. Teacher Kwu wrote a letter to Dr. Morrison describing his experience in the following terms:

"The moral disease of man in this world is ignorance of his true condition and too great a compliance with the customs of the world. During the last few months I have fallen in with my religious elder brother, and have been with him morning and evening listening to the Truth. He says the great source of Truth is from Heaven—that ancient doctrines, though diverging through many channels, all revert to one God. On hearing this I was suddenly awakened, and began to think of my former sins, stains, and pollutions. I desired to seek the gate of pardon, but knew not, the way thither. Happily I found the hand of my religious elder brother pointing the way. He said 'Though your sins be as heavy as the Great Mountain, if you truly repent, reform, and trust in Jesus the Savior of the world, you will obtain the blotting out of your sins and gain everlasting life!' I therefore poured out my heart reverently, believed, and received the rite of baptism to cleanse away the filth of sin, hoping for the grace of the Holy Spirit to implant in my heart a root of holiness, and assist me in bringing forth the fruit of holy virtue."[3] This confession of faith by the young pilgrim is a striking testimony to the competence of his guide.

The friendship between Teacher Kwu and A-fa led to a new experiment. The two opened a Christian school for boys in their district. This was the first venture in Protestant education within China. The evangelist made use of the traditional respect the Chinese have always had for the teacher and the school to promote the work of evangelism. The whole subsequent history of missions has borne witness to the worthwhileness of this method. Not only did it find an opportunity in the impressionable years of childhood, and through the natural contacts with parents and other relatives, to introduce Christian truth, but at the same time it conferred the universally appreciated gift of education on the children. It was a demonstration of what the Christians thought of the importance of learning, and proved the essential harmony between ancient Chinese culture and the Christian religion. But the time had not arrived when such an innovation could pass unchallenged. After a few months opposition was stirred up. It was said that A-fa was disseminating a wicked superstition, and that his purpose was to sell China to the foreigners who employed him. The school was broken up, and A-fa had to flee for his life to the shelter of Macao. Nothing further is known of Teacher Keu.

Liang A-fa was welcomed by Dr. Morrison and continued his studies and literary work. In reporting A-fa's work for that year (1828) to the Society Dr. Morrison mentions the writing of twelve tracts, one of them a catechism for children used in his village school. Another answered certain objections made to Christianity by his friends. A sample will show what they were like. One was "Since the Savior is said to be Lord of earth and heaven, and possessed of infinite power, and nothing was impossible to Him, why did He debase Himself by entering the womb and being born into the world a human being, thus defiling and degrading the most holy Divine nature? Such a statement is greatly inconsistent with truth and reason." Another: "Since the Gospel is so fine a doctrine, and God has almighty power, why does He not convert the Emperor, and cause him to order that it be received, instead of employing such mean persons as you are?' And again: "Since Jesus did not appear before the time of the Han dynasty how could He save those who lived before that period, and how can He be called the Savior of the world?" In his book A-fa answered the various questions and objections, and also related some conversations with people of different classes. Some of these greeted his zeal for this new and strange doctrine with smiles, others became angry at his criticisms of idolatry, while others again were willing to admit the truth and reasonableness of his statements, but considered the opinions attacked so deeply rooted in the nature of the Chinese as to defy all efforts at eradication. By such methods this pioneer in Christian literature distribution kept his product in touch with live problems. Dr. Morrison was much impressed with the value of these tracts, expressing the opinion that no European writer in Chinese could equal their author in effectiveness. Two of the tracts were in metrical form, an arrangement very popular in China because it lends itself to singing and is easily remembered.

Early in 1830 another disciple was added to the little group. This was Kew A-gong (in Cantonese Wat Ngong) who had been taught the printing trade at Malacca by Liang A-fa, and worked in the mission press there for some years. When he returned to China he continued to do printing for Dr. Morrison and was thus under regular Christian instruction. He had formerly led an idle life, and neglected to provide for his wife and family. His village home was in the vicinity of Whampoa, at that time Canton's port for overseas shipping, and some ten miles from the city. When baptized by Dr. Morrison in his house at Macao he at once returned home and urged his wife to desist from idolatry and trust in Jesus alone for the pardon of sins. As it was mainly through A-fa's influence that A-gong became a Christian, we can readily surmise that this first step in witnessing to his new faith was A-fa's suggestion. But A-gong was perhaps too precipitate and his wife was not so tractable as A-fa's had been. His past behavior had not encouraged her affection and confidence. When he knelt to pray in the home without the usual incense sticks and candles, and not before the family tablets or idols, she reproached him for worshipping the foreigner's gods. She carried her complaint to her neighbors, and publicly railed at him as a renegade, saying that his prayers brought her bad luck as it had rained on her washing day! A-gong, finding his home too hot for him, joined A-fa as assistant in his evangelistic and literary work. After this apprenticeship he was engaged the following year by the London Missionary Society and remained in their employment until his death at a ripe old age. He became a most faithful and valuable worker.

As already mentioned there is preserved in the Society's archives in London a journal written by Liang A-fa recording his work from March 28 until November 6, 1830. For a great part of that time A-gong was associated with A-fa, six weeks being spent together in a return trip between Canton and Kochau—a journey of about 800 miles. Before setting out on this tour the pair went to A-fa's home in Koming, and there prepared and printed the tracts to be used in this work. The preparation of the literature, however, was much less important than the preparation of the workers, and the journal shows A-fa passing through a very definite spiritual experience before setting out.

There is evidence that something else beside his friend A-gong's conversion had greatly stirred the evangelist's soul. The many appeals from Morrison had at last brought a practical response from the churches in America, and the Revs. E. C. Bridgman and D. Abeel arrived in Canton in February. Bridgman was to labor among the Chinese, while Abeel was to fill the place of seamen's chaplain at Whampoa. On March 25 Dr. Morrison invited these brethren to meet Liang A-fa at his rooms. Both of the American missionaries used the words "He bears the image of the Lord Jesus Christ" as summing up their first impression of this Chinese disciple.[4] Before parting A-fa read in Chinese the tenth chapter of St. Luke and spoke briefly on the second verse: "The harvest is plenteous but the laborers are few; pray ye therefore the Lord of the harvest that He send forth laborers into His harvest."[5] Bridgman remarks: "If the same ideal and impressions which he expressed in regard to this verse were generally entertained by Christians the laborers would not be so disproportioned in number to the extensive harvest."[6] Then they all knelt while A-fa led in prayer, Dr. Morrison translating the meaning into English before they rose from their knees. The prayer was no formal utterance, but full of genuine emotion and sincerity, as well as being adapted to their special circumstances. That first Sino-American-British missionary prayer meeting in 1830 might well appeal to some Christian artist as the subject for a historic picture. It was the beginning of a wonderful partnership that continues today. Thus the two new missionaries were welcomed into the Church in China and received a further seal of their ordination and commission from the heart and lips of Liang A-fa. Abeel wrote in his journal that evening before retiring to rest: "If the promise respecting the Jews be applicable to the Chinese, and the multitude composing the lump be individually as holy as the first fruits (Romans 11:16), we may expect a glorious harvest from this neglected part of the Savior's vineyard. . . . The feelings he expressed in welcoming missionaries to his benighted country were awakened in us at the sight of one in whom appeared so distinctly the image of the Savior."[7] But the incident had also its strong reaction on the mind of the evangelist himself. He felt that the reinforcement of workers from abroad was a challenge to him as a Chinese believer. A few days later he went back to see Dr. Morrison and said: "I have been a believer in the Savior for several years but have never yet done anything worthy for God. If I should suddenly die and God asked me what I had done what could I say? I wish to take A-gong and go everywhere distributing Scriptures and tracts and preaching the Gospel. This is our purpose, but we have not sufficient money for our travelling expenses." Morrison promised to give the money needed and advised him to be cautious and not run into needless danger. A-fa asked the missionary to continually pray that God would protect and guide them. Then they knelt together and committed this new enterprise to the Lord of the harvest. A-gong and A-fa went first to the village home in Lohtsun to prepare for their trip. One day when reading his Bible A-fa came to a passage which he often quotes: "How then shall they call on him in whom they have not believed? and how shall they believe in him of whom they have not heard? and how shall they hear without a preacher? and how shall they preach except they be sent?"[8] After reading it he thought again of God's grace in his conversion and opportunity of study, and the task committed to him of preaching the Gospel. How could his people learn its meaning if he did not teach them? There and then he made up his mind to study the Scriptures more diligently that he might be better fitted. The next day he began with Genesis and was so moved by the story of the creation that he knelt down and prayed for the Holy Spirit's light on such mysteries. He wrote in his journal: "If I can always keep the eyes of my heart fixed on this purpose to study the Bible and never forget it I can become a preacher." He went on to read the whole Bible and completed it in ten days.

When a sufficient number of tracts had been prepared by the two printer evangelists, they returned to Canton and discussed the direction of their tour. At first they thought of travelling North. Finally they decided to visit the office of the Literary Chancellor, who supervised the literary examinations throughout the province, visiting each of the prefectural cities in turn, and find out where he was going next. What led A-fa to this momentous decision we do not know. He changed his plans for going North because a fellow traveler on the passage boat who had offered to guide them on their journey, and to whom A-fa had given a small advance payment, disappeared after he got the bargain money. A-gong had a relative in the Literary Chancellor's retinue and this may have influenced them. The main reason, however, for turning his attention to the literati was a growing conviction, by which the evangelist recognized the leading of the Divine Spirit, that Christianity could only win its way among his people under educated leadership. Conscious of his own limitations and of the crudities of style inevitable in books written or translated by non-Chinese, he hoped through the means of even such admittedly imperfect material to secure the conversion to Christ of men whose scholarship and literary ability would command the attention both of their fellows and the common people. With this purpose the evangelist and his assistant, their boxes of literature carried by passage boat and barrow, followed the Chancellor nearly four hundred miles to Kochow. They distributed books in the different markets through which they passed en route. Arrived at their destination, and having received the cordial sanction of the authorities through A-gong's relative, they took their stand day after day at the entrance to the examination hall and gave their books to the students as they left. In this way several hundreds of the aspirants for the literary degree carried the printed message back to their homes. Kochow has long been famed as a progressive literary centre and today—over a century later—a young graduate of the Union Theological College at Canton has just taken up special work among students there. A-fa was so much encouraged by their success that he decided to advance the offensive right to the central citadel of the enemy. The two friends returned to Canton, and after preparing a further supply of ammunition, continued the distribution of their books at the provincial examination hall in the centre of this metropolis of South China.

Illustration 7.1 Photograph of a letter written by Liang A-fa on September 18, 1827, still preserved in the archives of the London Missionary Society, London.

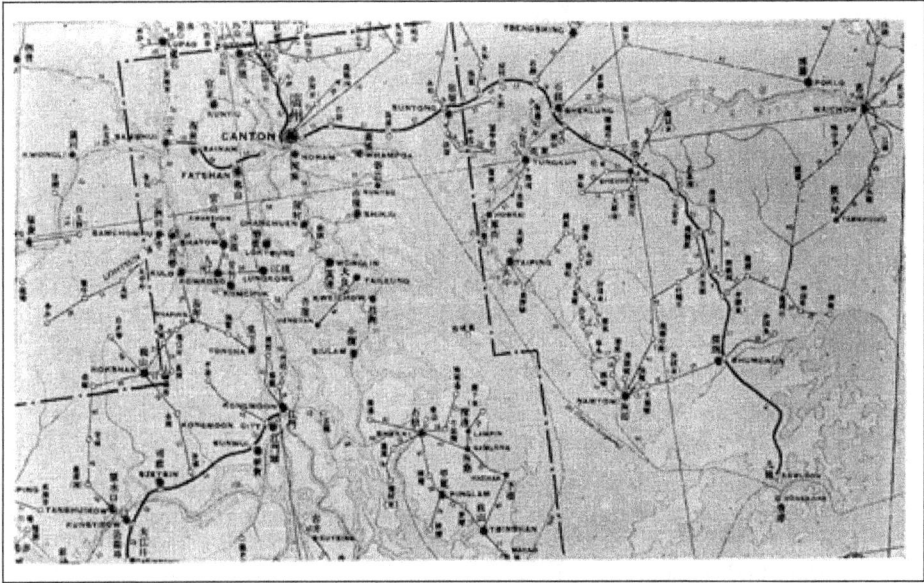

Illustration 7.2 Lohtsun, the birthplace of Liang A-fa is South-West from Canton. Hong Kong is in the lower right hand corner. (From the Chinese Postal Map of Kwangtung Province)

Notes

1. Temple Gairdner (1873–1928) was a famous Anglican scholar-missionary, known for developing an Arabic apologetics. This quote is presumably from the work published just a few years earlier, Constance E. Padwick, *Temple Gairdner of Cairo* (London: Society for Promoting Christian Knowledge, 1929).

2. This is part of the LMS collection now housed within the CWM collection at London University, School of Oriental and African Studies and available on microfilm from IDC.

3. This is an abridged letter cited in Walter Medhurst, *China: Its State and Prospects*, 274. The original appears to be "Keuteëching to Dr. Morrison," *The Evangelical Magazine and Missionary Chronicle* VI (Nov. 1828), 495. In this earlier version, Kwu's letter was published along with several other small entries: a letter from Morrison, a letter from Liang, a prayer of thanksgiving, and a short translation.

4. David Abeel, *Journal of a Residence in China and the Neighboring Countries* (New York: J. Abeel Williamson, 1836), 116.

5. Ibid. In both this and the preceding case, McNeur provides quotes where Abeel only summarized. The original spoke of "the image of the Savior" and said that he "read the tenth chapter of Luke in Chinese, and explained with much propriety the passage, respecting the harvest and laborers."

6. Eliza J. Gillett Bridgman, *The Life and Labours of Elijah Coleman Bridgman* (New York: Anson D. F. Randolph, 1864), 43.

7. David Abeel, *Journal of a Residence in China and the Neighboring Countries* (New York: J. Abeel Williamson, 1836), 115.

8. Romans 10:14–15a (King James Version).

8

Individual Evangelism

"Personal contact of a friend, or a Christian worker, or a relative, wins far more persons to Christianity than any other one method, and almost as many as all other methods combined."[1]

—*RE-THINKING MISSIONS*

The picture of Liang A-fa's natural disposition drawn by his earlier missionary associates is not very attractive. Milne speaks of him as "not so sociable and engaging as that of many other Chinese."[2] Morrison found "his natural temper irritable and hasty, and his address unengaging to his fellow-countrymen." This must have been a serious handicap to his usefulness, but subsequent testimony indicates a gradual change for the better with ripening Christian experience. A-fa naturally reflected the somewhat over-serious type of evangelical Christianity represented by the earlier missionaries—both British and American. They seem to have somehow missed the truth that "the kingdom of God is also joy." There is little sense of humor and grace of laughter in the portraits history has handed down to us. One would be as hard put to it to find biographical materials for a chapter entitled "In lighter moods" on Robert Morrison as he would be in describing Liang A-fa. True Morrison did as a lad join himself to a company of strolling play actors, but a biographer considers this the last role for which he was fitted, "he being the most stolid of men and almost, if not entirely, devoid of humor."[3]

Any occasional glimpse we get of A-fa in his own home show us a man of strong natural affections. He was a dutiful son and a loving husband and father. The journal mentioned in the previous chapter contains frequent references to his home relationships. It was his custom on arriving at his house after an absence to gather the family for worship, giving thanks to God for His protecting care during their separation.

When A-gong and he had to set out on their dangerous inland mission he tried to prepare their minds by explaining to his wife and little son the tenth chapter of St. Matthew, telling them how the Savior when on earth sent his disciples everywhere to preach the Gospel and was now sending them in the same way. They must not be anxious, as they were engaged in God's business and He would watch over them. On the Sunday before leaving he conducted the customary two sessions of worship in the home. In the morning he directed their attention to Acts 14: 32, where it is said the disciples returned to the places where they had already suffered persecution, "confirming the souls of the disciples, exhorting them to continue: in the faith, and that through many tribulations we must enter into the kingdom of God."[4] At noon he reminded them of the battle-cry of the Apostle Paul as he began his mission in Corinth, that wicked city: "I determined not to know anything among you save Jesus Christ and Him crucified."[5] Thus he sought to comfort his family, to teach and inspire his companion, and to feel afresh the urge of his own commission from his Lord. On the Monday morning the two men set out in true apostolic fashion, along the top of the Samchow flood dyke, on their first missionary journey.

Another illuminating insight is afforded us when, after A-fa returned home, the people around were celebrating the propitiatory rites for the souls of the dead customary to the fifteenth day of the seventh moon. Some years earlier the evangelist had poured out his soul to Morrison regarding the observance of this festival. He wrote: "When I look on such stupid nonsense I am exceedingly grieved and at a loss what to do. I can only meditate and give heed to my own conduct continually, carefully and firmly holding to the Truth, and, looking up, pray to the Lord on high to convert the hearts of men."[6] This time he discussed the matter with his wife. After speaking of the way in which rich and poor alike were deluded by the priests he went on: "In spite of the serious economic results everyone is happy to take part. When I urge people not to do this wickedness and waste their money I am railed at by them."[7] His wife said: "Who among the people of today can differentiate between what is wrong and what is right? What the crowd is happy to do each individual wishes to do. We are not willing to follow the crowd in burning incense and paper money and candles, and so

I constantly hear them say of you, 'He talks like a Roman Catholic' or 'He vilifies the gods and spirits, and will certainly suffer some great calamity!' A-fa asked "Do you share the idea of these people that because I exhort them not to worship idols some calamity will come upon me?" The wife replied: "My wish is that there will be no calamity. All I fear is that we two— husband and wife—may not be able to keep all God's commandments and thus suffer calamity." A-fa said "You are right. But sometimes God allows His servants to suffer hardship in order that their hearts may be awakened, and that they may be taught there is no place of rest and blessedness in this world. They must wait for that until the life to come, when their souls shall enjoy true happiness in Heaven. You must have a patient heart and try to be good, trusting in the grace of our Lord and Savior and hoping for that happiness. Thus will your heart always be kept in peace."

Tsen-teh had already a little sister named A-chim ("Received") born in 1829. A fortnight after the festival mentioned above A-fa returned home from Canton just when another little one was hourly expected. It was only his keen sense of duty that had taken him away at such a critical time. Before leaving he had sought by the explanation of the third chapter of Genesis to show his wife the connection, as he saw it, between the suffering of the mother in childbirth and human sin. At the same time he assured her that through the redemptive merit of the Savior her sins had been forgiven and her soul was safe, come what might. He counseled her to pray constantly that God might have mercy on her and give her peace, promising on his part to think of her continually and return as quickly as possible. The brave wife replied "It is most important you should attend to God's business, You need not be anxious about me." The visit to Canton was for the purpose of leading a Mr. Lam, whom he had found an interested enquirer, to a definite decision.

When he entered his house on return and saw his wife's face he knew he was just in time to share her trouble. Learning from her that she was indeed in great pain he went up the ladder to the little attic study and kneeling down he besought God's help for his wife. When he had prayed he went down and comforted her heart. The entries in the journal for the following days reveal the distress and anxiety through which the home passed while the wife and mother went down into the valley of the shadow of death and then slowly struggled back to life and hope. It was a time of severe testing for the husband. One day he sat alone and meditated on the trouble and sorrow of mankind and the suffering through which his own wife was passing. He remembered that his money was all spent and even his clothes were in the pawnshop. His wife was still very ill and needed his constant attention. They could not afford to hire help. His conclusion was that it would be easier to die for the Gospel than to endure prolonged suffering.

A month later, after morning worship and breakfast, A-fa said to his wife "Tomorrow I have to go to Canton. You must take care of yourself and do not be anxious. Although you cannot see my face I shall certainly be praying day and night that God will take care of you." The following year the baby son, born in such sore travail, was taken Home.

At a time when the preaching of Christianity was a crime punishable by death conversational evangelism was the only possible method. There is abundant evidence that A-fa was faithful in his use of opportunities, however much his natural reticence and lack of social qualities may have added to his many other difficulties. Over a century ago he had discovered the truth of the quotation which introduces this chapter. The best way to illustrate the evangelist's way of doing personal work will be to take from his journal an account of his attempt to lead the Mr. Lam already mentioned to the Savior. Mr. Lam kept a boarding house in Canton at which the two preachers stayed when they returned from Kochow. The day after arrival Mr. Lam suddenly entered his boarder's room and found him praying. He asked in surprise "What god are you kneeling on the floor to worship?" A-fa replied "The God whom we worship is the Lord who in the beginning created the heaven and earth, spirits and men and all things, and governs the people of all nations. He is omnipresent and omniscient, the living God. Therefore wherever men pray to Him with a sincere heart He hears them." Mr. Lam's laconic comment on this explanation was "That is very convenient!"

Next day A-fa gave Mr. Lam two books, saying "Brother, when you have read these books do not be afraid to ask me about anything you do not understand. I shall do my best to explain." Mr. Lam thanked him and later came to his room to ask "Where does this book of the true Scriptures which you talk about come from? "A-fa told him "This book was originally preserved in the kingdom of the Jews. Formerly the people of that kingdom had little contact with those of other countries. They did not keep the law of God, but followed the customs of other lands in worshipping idols, doing a great many licentious and wicked things. Still God sent prophets and wise men to teach repentance from sin. Not only were they unwilling to listen, but they even seized their teachers, imprisoning some and killing others.

Therefore God moved other nations to send armies to destroy their capital city and country. Those who in their hearts believed in the true Scriptures and obeyed their doctrines had these happenings revealed to them beforehand. They were told to take the true Scriptures and escape to foreign lands, where they should preach the doctrine and exhort men. This is the reason that now all nations know of the doctrine in the true Scriptures. Several years ago I was working in a foreign country and there knew a good man who taught me from this book, and told me to take the message of the book and prepare tracts for distribution. The object in doing this is that men receiving the exhortation might not be so deceived by the devil as to fail in recognizing the fundamental doctrines regarding human origin and destiny, and lose their precious souls. Having been taught in this holy book I understand its mysteries to a certain extent." Mr. Lam said "So the holy book of the true Scriptures came originally from foreign countries. We Chinese follow all sorts of customs, and do not trouble to examine whether they are true or false. You have now come to my boarding house to stay, and surely Heaven has sent you to save us from our delusions." A-fa replied "You must yourself be willing to believe the doctrine of the true Scriptures with a sincere heart before you can be delivered from delusions. If you only half believe and half doubt then your loss will be the greater and your sin the heavier." The innkeeper said "I certainly believe the sacred teaching of the true Scriptures, but will you please explain it to me so that I may believe with my whole heart." The evangelist's comment on this request is interesting. He said "All who would believe in the holy Scriptures must believe first, and then only can they understand their teaching. You wish to understand first and believe afterwards. I am afraid you are not a sincere believer in the doctrine. The more you hear the more you will doubt, and the less likely are you to have a trusting heart." Mr. Lam said "My mind is already made up; I only wish you to teach me." Just then someone called the innkeeper away.

Two days later A-fa was reading in his room when Mr. Lam entered and asked "What does the book you gave me—'The Conversation between Two Friends'—mean by faith in Jesus?" A-fa said "Jesus is the holy Son of God. To believe in Him means to believe that He suffered and died to redeem mankind from sin, that He possesses the almighty power of God to save men's souls and after death to give them everlasting life, and that He can by the Holy Spirit transform the hearts of wicked men, making them good. That is what faith in Jesus means." Mr. Lam then retired.

Again A-fa was studying alone when the innkeeper appeared to ask what kind of a person Jesus was. A-fa told him "The name Jesus in the Scriptures means 'the Savior of the world.' In His human nature He suffered and died to redeem mankind from sin. After death and burial for three days and nights He was able to rise again in His Divine nature and later ascend to Heaven. Thus He is able to save the souls of all who believe in Him from the torments of hell."

About a week later Mr. Lam came to A-fa's room and said with great joy, "I have read 'The Explanation of the True Doctrine' and have also listened to your teaching, and I find much delight in it. Please tell me how the Savior of the world suffered death to redeem men from sin, and how He saves men's souls." A-fa replied "I could not tell you all about the mysterious doctrine of the suffering and death of the Savior for the redemption of men from sin if I talked for a whole year. But I shall attempt to give you a general idea. Why should the Savior, who had not the slightest sin, suffer even to death? God, because of His love and compassion for the world, took the punishment men should suffer and caused the Savior to bear it on man's behalf. Thus all who realize their sin are enabled to repent and believe in the Savior Jesus, and because of the merit of His death they are saved punishment and receive the forgiveness of sins. This is the general meaning of the expression 'redemption from sin.' The salvation of the soul by the Savior begins with conviction of sin by the Holy Spirit and the changing of the nature to goodness. Then the Savior helps men in their hearts to gain victory over the temptations of the devil, guiding them throughout their lives to keep God's law. At death, on account of the great merit of the Savior being reckoned as their merit, their souls escape the torments of hell and are granted the enjoyment of heaven's blessedness. This is the general meaning of the expression 'salvation of the soul.' Therefore it is written 'He that believes in the Savior shall receive happiness, but he that is unwilling to believe shall suffer everlasting woe.' Mr. Lam said "Now I understand the meaning of the true Scriptures more clearly. Today I am busy, but another day I shall come and learn more."

A-fa was praying in his room that God would send His Holy Spirit to convert the hearts of those who had heard the teaching when Mr. Lam again came to see him. A-fa said to him "Those who wish to learn the teaching of God's true Scriptures must do two things. They must give earnest heed to the teaching they have heard, considering the comparative length and brevity of the woe or happiness coming to body and soul. Most important of all, Mr. Lam, you must when alone pray God to give His Holy Spirit for the conversion of your heart, causing you to know your sins, the value of the soul, the dangers of this world, the nature of eternal happiness after death, and the sorrows of those who suffer eternal woe. Pray too that He may teach you how the Savior can redeem you from sin, deliver you from the bitterness of eternal woe, and lead you into the way of everlasting peace. If you set your mind on these things you may obtain the grace of God's Holy Spirit to convert your heart." Mr. Lam said "My mind is at present much confused. Before I met you I wished to become a Buddhist priest, and paid several visits to the monastery. The priests welcomed me, but when they discovered my parents had a certain amount of wealth they were unwilling to shave my head until my father and brothers had given permission." A-fa replied "How fortunate you did not become a Buddhist priest. You are indeed a lucky man! If you had embraced the Buddhist religion you would have entered the gates of hell." Mr. Lam asked "Why do you say that?" A-fa said "The Buddhist priests deceive people in many ways. They say if one son leaves the home to become a priest nine ancestors will ascend to heaven. Just ask the priest by what merit these ascend to heaven. Not only are the priests today unable to enter heaven, but even Buddha himself was a great sinner. Not to mention any other sin he was unwilling to reverently recognize [before] God. For that sin of rebellion he deserves eternal punishment. Buddha was born during the Chow dynasty on the confines of China. Even if it be granted he lived a virtuous life, an examination of the Buddhist sacred books will show that they do not speak of his virtue being of benefit to anyone. They only tell you if you would enter the Buddhist religion you must sit in abstract meditation looking on the image of Buddha and reciting the sacred books. Let me ask whether sitting in abstract meditation benefits Buddha or any other person? How can anyone, even if sinless himself, by entering the Buddhist religion and doing nothing all day but recite prayers and meditate, benefiting nobody, remove the anger of the gods, release from sin, and by his merit ascend to heaven and enjoy eternal bliss? They say too that by studying the sacred books and reciting prayers you can go to India in the West, the land of Buddha, and enjoy that place of great felicity. But you can go to India without studying sacred books and reciting prayers to Buddha. If you have money enough to pay your fare you can go there on a ship. The tricks of these Buddhists and their sacred books are used to cheat people out of their money in order that the priests themselves may sit in laziness and enjoyment. How can such people, full of sin, for whom execution is too good, hope to ascend to heaven?" To this scathing indictment Mr. Lam replied "In my former ignorance I thought it a good thing to become a Buddhist. Who would have known, if you had not told them, that this would be so great a sin? But the priests have many good things to say about their religion." "Naturally," said A-fa, "they have to talk of its good features in order to attract people and get their money. They deceive men into becoming Buddhists in order to satisfy their own villainous hearts. Before I was converted by God, when ignorant of the true Scriptures, I also wished to become a Buddhist. But later, when God in His grace changed my heart, and I knew, believed and obeyed the mysteries of the true Scriptures, I knew the harm of Buddhism and the value of the Scriptures and the holy religion. I have already told you something about the mysteries of the true Scriptures, and whether you believe or not rests with yourself. But whatever you do, do not become a Buddhist priest, because if you follow Buddha there will be no end to your troubles." Mr. Lam said "I now know the harm of Buddhism and the benefit of belief in the true Scriptures. But there is something in my heart which hinders me from as yet seeking baptism. Later I shall take time to tell you about it." Having said this he went out.

Soon after A-fa had to return home. He found the innkeeper so grateful for his teaching that he was at first unwilling to take rent for his room, and only accepted the money on condition that when A-fa returned to the city he would stay with him as his guest. Mr. Lam said "Your teaching is after my own heart, and your words and actions are such that people respect you."

It would double the length of this chapter to give in detail the continued dialogue on the next visit, A-fa immediately began with constructive teaching, using specially the epistle of St. James. Every day, morning and evening, he opened his own heart and the Scriptures to his friend, but left him still undecided. In a few weeks, however, he was back again to resume his teaching. And now at last Mr. Lam's real difficulty came out. One day he said "I believe every word you say, but I do not dare to receive baptism because my father's business is the selling of paper materials. (Much of this material is used in idolatrous ceremonies.) If I am baptized and profess faith in Jesus I cannot engage in this business." He wished to be a secret disciple, making no open confession unless his father consented to his baptism. This evasion was met with the Lord's words "He that loveth father and mother more than me is not worthy of me." A-fa pointed out he would be guilty of unfilial conduct if he made his father's business an excuse for shirking his duty to God and man. Basing his remarks on the Lord's words "If any man would come after me let him deny himself and take up his cross and follow me" and the following verses A-fa made an earnest appeal for decision. He said: "In these verses Jesus taught His disciples that if any man wishes to believe in the Truth he must be willing to overcome his own desires and put away completely all the evil customs of the world. He must be ready to suffer pain and hardship, imprisonment and death before he can follow Christ."

Thus the evangelist preached the Word, instant in season, out of season, reproving, rebuking, exhorting, with all long suffering and teaching. The result in this case was that the innkeeper finally became a Christian and was baptized by Liang A-fa the following year.

Notes

1. William Ernest Hocking, *Re-thinking Missions: A Laymen's Inquiry After One Hundred Years* (New York: Harper & Brothers Publishers, 1932), 99. *Re-thinking Missions* was an international effort to evaluate Protestant missions, chaired by Hocking, a philosophy professor at Harvard. A major influence in the fundamentalist-modernist controversy, it provoked a range of responses.

2. William Milne, *A Retrospect of the First Ten Years of the Protestant Mission to China* (Malacca: Anglo-Chinese Press, 1820), 178.

3. Marshall Broomhall, *Robert Morrison: A Master Builder* (London: Student Christian Movement, 1927), 13.

4. King James Version.

5. 1 Corinthians 2:2 (King James Version).

6. Elizabeth A. Morrison, *Memoirs of the Life and Labours of Robert Morrison,* 2:407.

7. This and subsequent quotes are translations from Liang's 1830 *Diary of Words and Deeds* (*Riji yanxing*), a handwritten account of his printing work, evangelistic trips, and life in the Canton area: Liang Fa, *Riji yanxing* [A Diary of Words and Deeds] (n.p.: 1830). The diary is part of the IDC CWM collection: H-2138:1–2 (Journals 1807–1842: Boxes 1-2:1830). I believe McNeur is the only author to have translated substantial portions of the journal.

9

A Double Blow

"Our friends in England seem to have given up the Chinese mission in China. When revolving in my mind which course to pursue I am hindered by the recollection that of late no measures seem even to have been thought of how the mission in China—that is the English mission—is to be continued in the event of my removal by any cause. . . . Oh what a treasury is the Bible. To turn over its pages and read of God's dealings with His people is quite refreshing to the soul."[1]

—Dr. Morrison, January 20, 1834

The period between 1831 and 1834 seems to have been the most fruitful in Liang A-fa's ministry at Canton. Not only did he receive into church fellowship Mr. Lam the innkeeper but also one of the boarders, a mason named Li San. Li became so earnest that he was later engaged as an assistant preacher. During 1831 four others were baptized, three of whom—a father and two sons—belonged to the literati. How many of these converts remained faithful we do not know. The cost of enduring to the end was greater than some were willing to pay. Dr. Hobson wrote at the time of A-fa's death "He has converted few, very few, and several whom he baptized many years ago he has seen lapse again into idolatry and sin." But their profession was a present encouragement to the evangelist, who wrote with joy, "There are more than ten of us who, with one heart and united mind, continually serve the Lord. Every Sabbath day we assemble together to praise the Savior for the mighty grace of redemption."[2]

There were other things besides this fruit of his preaching that cheered the lonely evangelist. His boy Tsen-teh was taken by Mr. Bridgman into his own home for teaching. The missionary gave him regular lessons in English, so that at the age of twelve he was able to read the Scriptures in that language as well as in Chinese. He was also taught some Hebrew and Greek in the hope he might be thus equipped to prepare a more perfect translation of the Bible. The father rejoiced that his son was so privileged, and constantly prayed he might become a minister of the Gospel. He found encouragement too in the changed attitude of his father, who became willing to admit the God of the Scriptures was the true God, and joined in family worship. But he still continued to worship the gods of his people, protesting in defense that he could not presume to think himself wiser than the emperor and officials who worshipped them. Dr. Morrison mentions that on one occasion A-teh was very ill, his parents despairing of his life. A-fa wrote down the names of several doctors known to him and prayed that God would guide him which to invite. He then chose at random one of the paper slips which had the name of a Dr. Loo on it. Under his treatment the lad quickly recovered. When the grandfather saw what had happened he was convinced this God must be true and fell down and worshipped Him. On receiving this news in a letter from A-fa Dr. Morrison wrote in his journal "I suppose A-fa imitated what is recorded in Acts 1:24 when the disciples prayed and implored God to show which He had chosen. I am at a loss whether to condemn the transaction or not, for I dare not limit the Holy One of Israel." But the old father never made a final and full decision. Like the Samaritans of old he "feared Jehovah and served graven images."[3]

The encouragement A-fa received in a growing church and other ways increased his earnestness—and boldness. Dr. S. Wells Williams, on his first arrival at Canton in 1833, met the evangelist, and writes of his printing over 70,000 tracts and Scripture portions in one year. He says "He is now engaged in making books as fast as he can, and has distributed many thousands. A short time since there was an examination of literary candidates in Canton, and more than 25,000 candidates came. Liang A-fa got some coolies to take his boxes into the hall, and there he dealt out the Word of Life to intelligent young men as fast as he could handle the books. This he did three days together. He is a venerable looking old man about fifty years of age. His countenance expresses benevolence, and at first view you are prepossessed." About the same date Dr. Morrison writes "A-fa says in a letter that his mind is made up to all consequences. He is prepared for persecution, but up to the time of writing has remained in peace. A-fa's mind is very much excited to work while it is today. Awful calamities have this year befallen Canton province from water-inundations of rivers and windy storms. Many thousands have been drowned or crushed to death by falling houses, or starved and perished in consequence of being without shelter and food. A-fa's house among the rest was washed away. Throughout the whole of China, in the north by drought and scarcity, in the south by rain and inundation, in some places by sword and spear, and in the imperial harem by the death of the Empress, there has been a dread and gloom diffused over the land." Morrison was in constant anxiety for the safety of his intrepid fellow-worker. Writing of his venture at the examination hall he says "It is as bold a measure as for a tract distributor to go to the gownsmen at Oxford or Cambridge." The missionary had to find some comparison which would be appreciated by his readers in England. But the distributor, at British universities would hardly be running the risk of the Tower and the headman's block. Possibilities which would have daunted and dismayed most Chinese, because they are naturally timid, simply spurred A-fa to more courageous activity.

The reference to the quantity of literature distributed, raises the question of its nature and source. A book of Scripture lessons published in England for schools, and consisting of carefully selected passages of Scripture without note or comment, was produced in Chinese by using the same passages from the Chinese Bible. This was printed at Canton under the supervision of Liang A-fa. The cost of the first edition was subscribed by foreign residents in Canton, and later editions were paid for by the British and American Bible and Tract Societies. Each book was in a set of three volumes. These were not only given to the students, but A-fa carried them into the country around Canton, along with copies of a little magazine published by Morrison. He also used his own and other tracts, travelling expenses for longer trips being provided through Bridgman. Thus British and American Christians united in supplying A-fa with the sinews of war, but it was A-fa alone who risked his life to make their cooperation effective.

For some time previous to 1834 there had been symptoms that Dr. Morrison's health was failing. His wife and family—with the exception of the eldest living son John, who had been appointed Chinese translator to the British merchants in Canton at the early age of sixteen—sailed for England towards the end of 1833. In extreme loneliness and increasing weakness he continued his duties. On Feb. 5, 1834, he wrote in his journal "The sight of the children's chairs, etc., makes me very sad. My beloved children! Oh, when shall I again hear your prayers and kiss your cheeks?

My aching head! my aching head! Oh God, be merciful to me." Forty days before his death he prepared his last sermon, most appropriately on the words "In my Father's house are many mansions." He had been asked to preach in the East India Company's chapel at Macao by Lady Napier, wife of the British Ambassador, to whose embassy he was appointed as interpreter. But an objection was raised by some narrow-minded sectarian, and no service at all was considered better than one conducted by a minister who was regarded as not regularly ordained. The message at any rate reached his own heart, and on the last Sunday evening of his life he met with the little Chinese congregation in his house at Canton, where he may well have preached the same sermon. It was perhaps the largest gathering of the kind he had ever been privileged to see. In spite of great weakness and pain his heart was cheered as he ministered to them, specially when old Mr. Le, one of his writers, told him he had put his trust in Jesus. This Mr. Le is the sitting figure in the well-known portrait of Dr. Morrison with two Chinese assistants painted by Chinnery in 1829. In all probability A-fa—his friend and colleague—was present. They sang together the hymn "Jesus, lover of my soul" which Morrison had just recently translated. We can imagine the pioneer, when his congregation had dispersed and he was left alone, saying "Now lettest thou thy servant depart, O Lord, according to thy word, in peace." A few days later, at ten o'clock on the evening of the first of August 1834, the prayer was answered.

This fresh and poignant token of life's brevity incited Liang A-fa to even more daring activity. In less than three weeks he was back at the entrance to the great examination hall with his books. It was the triennial examination, to which candidates for the coveted degree gathered from all parts of the province. The hall contained 11,616 small cells in which the candidates were locked while they wrote their essays. The grounds are now occupied by the Chung-shan University.

There were circumstances that made A-fa's boldness exceptionally risky. The visit of Lord Napier to the city as Britain's Ambassador in an attempt to place Britain's trade and political relations with China on a more satisfactory footing had drawn attention to foreigners generally, and the British in particular. In fact trade relations with Britain had been severed on the sixteenth of August, owing to the insistence of Lord Napier that he should be permitted to communicate directly with the Viceroy. The Chinese Government would only allow him to use the customary medium of the Chinese hong merchants. All Chinese associated with the British, and specially those connected with the interpreter for the diplomatic mission—the late Dr. Morrison—were naturally suspect. A-fa knew this, but he willingly accepted the risk for his Master's sake. Like the ox standing between the plough and the altar he was ready for either. We have a detailed account of what happened from his own pen but it is too long to quote. Throughout the two first days of the examinations he and three assistants distributed thousands of books to the students without any trouble. On the third day one of the assistants was arrested by a police officer and taken with a set of the books to the magistrate. When he had examined the books the magistrate told the policeman not to interfere in such a small matter, and the assistant returned to his task. But on the fourth day the police came and seized A-fa, along with ten sets of the books. On the way to the Ya-men A-fa broke away from his captor and escaped to his home. He knew his experience in the same place some thirteen years before would lead to his getting short shrift now. The following day A-fa heard the matter had been carried to a higher court—that of the Governor—and fearing arrest he and his associates put the remaining books in boxes and removed them to another place. A-fa then left the city for his country home. A few days later the Governor sent soldiers to the house he had occupied in the city, where they arrested two of his helpers. When one of these pleaded ignorance he was beaten on the face until he was unable to speak. The other then told all he knew and the Governor proceeded to arrest those still in the city and neighboring villages who had taken part in the printing and distribution. They searched in vain however for the leader. When A-fa heard what was happening he left his village with his wife and daughter and fled to Kongmoon. Next day two military boats with a hundred soldiers arrived at Samchow with orders for quarry; they seized three of his relatives and sealed up his house. Cattle, pigs and fowl were carried off, as was the way of soldiers. After scouring the neighboring market and villages without result they returned to the city. News reached A-fa of what had transpired, and he left Kongmoon for the more secluded market of Chikhom. When he had exhausted his money he directed his wife to seek help from Dr. Bridgman at Canton. But on arrival she found Dr. Bridgman had gone to Macao. A-fa then took his family to Kongmoon and himself set out on the hazardous journey to Macao. He wrote "Thanks to the protecting mercy of God I reached Macao in safety, and when I met Dr. Bridgman the sorrow of my heart was so extreme that I could not refrain from weeping bitterly."[4] Dr. Bridgman told him Mr. J. R. Morrison had ascertained: that if $800 was paid to the Governor those arrested would be released, and he and his family would be pardoned. Taking money back to his wife with this encouraging news he again returned to Macao, where he stayed in Bridgman's house. Morrison wrote to say that while it was true the others would be released for $800 the Governor insisted on the arrest and punishment of Liang A-fa. This large sum was paid by Morrison and those still in prison were set at liberty. Dr. Bridgman took A-fa with his son A-teh in a fast boat to Lintin Island where he committed them to the friendly care of Captain Parry, in command of a British merchant ship.

It was while waiting for this ship to sail that he wrote the account of what had happened, closing with the words: "Thus situated I called to mind that all those who preach the Gospel of our Lord and Savior must suffer persecution. I therefore meditated on Romans 8:31–39, James 5:11 and 1 Peter 5:10, and though I cannot equal the patience of our Savior or of Paul or Job in enduring suffering, yet I desire to imitate the saints of ancient times and keep my heart in peace. Though I suffer severe persecution my heart finds some rest and joy, and my only fear now is lest the Chinese officers should injure my wife and daughter. I therefore, morning and evening, beseech God mercifully to protect and save them."[5]

With A-fa's account Messrs. Bridgman and Morrison sent a joint explanatory letter to the Mission. In it they point out that the charge against A-fa and his associates was not that of printing and distributing Christian books, but foreign books. It was because Lord Napier had taken the unprecedented method of posting up in the streets near the foreign factories lithographed notices in Chinese setting forth the British position. The authorities finding A-fa and his associates distributing books having a foreign connection, and discovering that A-fa himself had been in close touch with foreigners, suspected them of having been implicated in this matter. They were of course entirely innocent, but it would have been almost impossible for A-fa to prove this in face of his previous conviction and his long employment by a British mission of which Dr. Morrison, official interpreter for Lord Napier's commission, had been the head. From Lintin Liang A-fa and his son sailed for Singapore.

Illustration 9.1 Dr. Morrison with two Chinese assistants. From a painting by Chinnery in the Spring of 1829. (Neither of these is Liang A-fa, as has been wrongly supposed).

Illustration 9.2 From a Painting by George Chinnery of Dr. Peter Parker.

Notes

1. Elizabeth A. Morrison, *Memoirs of the Life and Labours of Robert Morrison,* 2:504.

2. David Abeel, *Journal of a Residence in China and the Neighbouring Countries from 1830–1833,* 90.

3. This is a paraphrase of 2 Kings 17:41, very similar to the American Standard Version.

4. Eliza J. Gillett Bridgman, ed., *The Life and Labor of Elijah Coleman Bridgman* (New York: Anson D. F. Randolph, 1864), 94.

5. Ibid., 95.

10

Wheat and Tares

"In the morning sow thy seed, and in the evening withhold not thy hand, for thou knowest not which shall prosper, whether this or that, or whether they both shall be alike good."

—ECCLESIASTES 2:6

It may be asked whether the brave and admittedly strategic efforts of the evangelist to reach and influence the literati were worthwhile. He himself was no scholar, and the literature he used had nothing in its style to commend it to the fastidious tastes of Chinese graduates. One answer to that question is the history of the Taiping rebellion. In that movement a set of Liang A-fa's tracts nearly turned China upside-down.

Before the distribution of books in front of the examination hall at Canton was hindered by the police in August 1834 a set of the tracts written by A-fa himself had been given to a young candidate named Hung Siu-tsuen. He failed to secure his degree, but carried back to his village in the Fa District, some twenty-five miles from the city, the package of Christian books. He paid little attention to them at the time, but placed them in a bookcase, where they lay unheeded for nine years. In 1837 he again tried his fortune at the triennial examination, and again failed. Shortly after this second attempt he became ill, and during convalescence had a series of remarkable visions. These continued for forty days and made a profound impression on his mind. In vision he saw a venerable old man who gave him a sword with which to exterminate demons. He saw also repeatedly a man of middle age whom he addressed as "Elder Brother," and who instructed him how to act.

Some years later (1843) he was in his room when visited by his wife's brother. The visitor called attention to the tracts lying in the bookcase. Hung took them out and began to read them. As he read he believed they provided the key to his visions. The venerable old man was the true God of whom the tracts spoke, and the Elder Brother was Jesus Christ. He immediately accepted his visions as Divine revelation and these books as providing their explanation. With a teacher friend named Fung Yun-san he began a campaign against idolatry. In spite of their intense earnestness their lack of the Christian knowledge necessary for any constructive program of reform made their attack on popular superstition rather futile. At last Hung decided to join forces with the Christians from whom the books had come. After another unsuccessful attempt at his degree in 1847 he went to visit the Rev. Issachar J. Roberts, an American Baptist missionary who resided on the river shore outside Tsing Hoi Gate, some distance from the factory area at Canton. Roberts was a remarkable man. Rev. Wm. Speer, one of the earliest missionaries of the American Presbyterian Church, says that during the year of Hung's visit Roberts was attending a Sunday evening service for the foreign community in Dr. Bridgman's house when a servant approached him while a hymn was being sung, and whispered in his ear that a band of fifty or sixty robbers was plundering his house. Speer was watching him, and not a muscle of his face moved to indicate his feelings. When he returned home next morning nothing remained but the brick walls. Even the windows, doors, and tiles from the floor had been carried off. Whether this happened before or after Hung came we do not know, but it was in that house and from the lips of this teacher that the young reformer received more detailed instruction in the Christian faith. After some weeks in the missionary's home he requested baptism. It is said that one of Roberts's Chinese assistants became afraid that Hung would be given his position, and so determined on a plan to get rid of him. He told him confidentially he would have to pay five dollars before he could be baptized. So Hung in his innocence went with the money to the missionary, who became as indignant as Peter had been when approached by Simon Magus, and probably used much the same language in rebuke. Roberts himself stated it was something the candidate said to him about employment after baptism that led him to delay administering the rite. He regretted the incident, but had great expectations from the later movement. That the reformer cherished no lasting sense of injury is proved by the fact that years later he invited his teacher to join his Government at Nanking as Minister for Foreign Affairs!

Roberts wrote on Christmas Day 1854: "I seriously believe the movement will be for the glory of God, also for the glory and benefit of China. If so who would not exult in the excellent effect."[1] But after spending fifteen months at the headquarters of the Taiping Government at Nanking he left completely disillusioned and bitterly disappointed.

When Hung was refused baptism he went out to found his own organization, which he called "The Society of God," and to enlist under his standard all who were ready to oppose the usurping Manchus and destroy the idols. In the neighboring province of Kwangsi he found a rebellious element of the populace ripe for his leadership, and before long he was at the head of a revolution which grew to gigantic proportions, and carried its victorious arms to within striking distance of Peking.

In Britain and America the news of this Christian Chinese patriot and his successful campaign aroused the liveliest hopes for the early conversion of the nation. The British and Foreign the Bible Society marked its jubilee by raising funds for the preparation and distribution of a million copies of the Scriptures in Chinese. The influence of Liang A-fa's books and Mr. Roberts' instruction was abundantly evident in the earlier stages of the movement. The insurgents themselves printed and circulated a version of the New Testament. Concerning one of their religious publications Dr. Medhurst could write: "This is decidedly the best production issued by the insurgents. The reasoning is correct, the prayers are good, and the statements of the doctrine of human depravity, redemption by the blood of Jesus, and renewal of the heart by the influence of the Holy Spirit are sufficient to direct any honest inquirer in the way to Heaven." The Ten Commandments and portions of the Sermon on the Mount were written in large characters and posted on the gates of Nanking. A cousin of the rebel leader and one of his principal officers named Hung Jin—known as the "Shield King"—had been an earnest evangelist in Hong Kong under the direction of Dr. Legge.

Unfortunately the success of his campaign brought disaster to the character of the leader. Never too strong mentally he became quite unbalanced. He formed an exaggerated estimate of his commission which betrayed him into blasphemous claims of semi-deity, and he fell a prey to all sorts of excesses. Dr. Wells Williams, writing some time after the suppression of the rebellion by the Government troops under the leadership of Chinese Gordon, said: "Ruined cities, desolated towns, and heaps of rubbish still mark their course from Kwangsi to Tientsin, a distance of 2,000 miles.

Their presence was an unmitigated scourge …….. Besides millions and millions of taels irrecoverably lost and destroyed, and the misery, sickness, and starvation which were endured by the survivors, it has been estimated that during the whole period from 1851 to 1865 fully thirty million beings perished in connection with the Taiping Rebellion."[2] Such a condemnatory statement by one so well qualified to judge leaves us in no doubt as to the final failure of the movement. But we need not shut our eyes to the spiritual and patriotic zeal with which it began, and which raised such high hopes for its success. The cruelty, corruption, and conservatism of the Manchu Government, and the degrading influences of superstition and idolatry, were enemies of China which deserved to be overthrown. Hung Siu-tsuen and his followers would have attained their objective, and opened the country to Christian culture, if they had remained obedient to the vision as it was interpreted by Liang A-fa's little tracts.

Regarding the effect of these books on the mind of the insurgent leader, Thomas Taylor Meadows, of the British Civil Service, has something to say in his book "The Chinese and their Rebellions" published in 1856: "Hung Siu-tsuen and his companion Fung Yun-san resolved to travel to another province as preachers, supporting themselves by selling ink and writing brushes because influenced by the words 'A prophet is not without honor save in his own country,' and by the notices of St. Paul's travels in Acts 19 given in Liang A-fa's books. If we examine A-fa's collection of pamphlets we find he deals only with subjects of the highest interest, and above all, of living interest to himself and his compatriots—e.g., the creation of the universe, the great moral rules of the Sermon on the Mount, and the proceedings and writings of St. Paul."[3] This is a valuable testimony from an unbiased source to the universality of Scripture teaching, and a striking commendation of Liang A-fa's choice of material. Mr. Meadows also pays a hearty tribute to the evangelist's earnestness and self-sacrifice. He criticizes his style, however, as based too much on the translation of the Bible and missionary tracts. This is hardly just, because A-fa quoted freely from Scripture, and naturally used the only translation then available. He was well aware that this needed revision and wrote: "The style adopted in the present version of the Scriptures is far from being idiomatic, the translators having sometimes used too many characters and employed inverted and unusual phrases, by which the sense is obscured. The doctrines of Scripture are in themselves deep and mysterious, and if in addition to this the style is difficult, men will be less likely to understand the book. I am a Chinese and know the style most suited to the Chinese mind. Let us endeavor therefore to render the version more idiomatic, and then print as many books as we please. The belief or rejection of the Scriptures rests with those to whom we deliver them, but it is our duty to render the sacred volume as intelligible as possible."[4]

The samples of A-fa's composition which have survived reveal a style closer to the simple form of expression popular in China today than to the intricate and difficult classical model favored by the scholars of the old school. If the pioneer in Christian literature had not the book learning necessary to win the approval of the stylists he could at least make his meaning reasonably clear to those who read his books. The effect was always much greater when he could follow up the reading with personal explanations. It is not surprising that much of his literary work proved to be as seed dropped on the hardened paths across the fields. Literature, and specially religious literature, however clear to the initiated, has always its difficulties for others. Even intelligent readers have usually to wait for a spoken interpretation of what they have read before it comes home to their hearts. Above all they need to see the "word made flesh" in some Christian character. As Sir Walter Scott makes his heroine Jeanie Deans say "Writing winna do it; a letter canna look, and pray, and beg, and beseech as the human voice can do to the human breast."[5] One cannot help wishing Hung Siu-tsuen had come to know Liang A-fa himself as well as his tracts.

Notes

1. Captain F. Brinkley, *China: Its History, Arts, and Literature* (Boston: J. B. Millet, 1902), vol. 11:236.

2. Samuel Wells Williams, *The Middle Kingdom, A Survey of the Geography, Government, Literature, Social Life, Arts, and History of the Chinese Empire and its Inhabitants, Vol. 2* (New York: Charles Scribner's Sons, 1907), 623. This is a later edition. S. Well Williams was an ABCFM missionary. This volume was first published in 1848 but substantially revised in 1882, adding this section on the Taiping.

3. This actually appears to be a combination of two quotes, with some revisions. The first tells of Hung and Fung's decision to travel and the second describes Liang's writings. Thomas Taylor Meadows, *The Chinese and Their Rebellions, Viewed in Connection with their National Philosophy, Ethics, Legislation, and Administration, to which is added, An Essay on Civilization and its Present State in the East and West* (London: Smith, Elder & Co., 1856), 84, 92.

4. Morrison's posthumously edited memoirs append an eighty-seven-page section, "Critical Notices of Dr. Morrison's Literary Labours, by Samuel Kidd (1804–1843), a London Missionary Society missionary and the first professor of Chinese in England." Kidd cites a version of this quote, written by Liang and included by Medhurst in a critical study of Morrison's translation: Elizabeth A. Morrison, *Memoirs of the Life and Labours of Robert Morrison*, 1:73.

5. From Walter Scott, *The Heart of the Midlothian*, originally published 1818.

11

Patriotism Not Enough

"Patriotism is often a cloak to conceal self-interest, or absence of reason and facts. Very tardily has the British public inscribed on Nurse Cavell's monument the words 'Patriotism is not enough.' Nurse Cavell was right; patriotism is not enough. Standing on the edge of two worlds she saw clearly that only in the full application of Christian brotherhood between men and nations was there any hope for the world."[1]

—KENNETH MACLENNAN

D r. Medhurst, of the London Missionary Society, visited Canton six months after Liang A-fa and his son sailed for the Straits Settlements, to enquire what had happened to the scattered flock of Christians. With Dr. Morrison dead, Liang A-fa exiled, and the authorities so alert in their opposition, the little church was in a sad plight. A literary graduate named Lew Tse-chuen, whom A-fa had baptized a year before, was the only one with whom Dr. Medhurst could get in touch. He was still assisting the American missionaries by revising the style of their tracts. This man was an interesting proof of what could happen—even in the case of a connoisseur in style—when the reading of Christian literature was supplemented by personal contact with an earnest Christian. A-fa had met him, and because the evangelist was always glad to get efficient help in making his books more acceptable, he engaged Mr. Lew to rewrite some of them. This work brought the graduate to A-fa's city home, and he attended worship mornings and evenings. When he began to argue with the preacher he found him able to answer all his objections. He had an impediment in his speech, so that most of the conversation on his part had to be carried on with pencil and paper. After some months of A-fa's teaching and friendship, and the reading of the books which he was revising, Mr. Lew suddenly woke as from a dream, and earnestly desired baptism. When Dr. Medhurst arrived this Christian came to see him in Mr. J. R. Morrison's rooms, and told him how the other members of the group had fared. It may be that Mr. Lew's standing as a scholar with a degree had protected him from active persecution.

One of the first men to be baptized by A-fa, a pen brush maker, by name Chow A-san, had saved his own skin by guiding the soldiers to the evangelist's village home. This man had been a great disappointment to his pastor, as it was evident his profession had not been genuine, but motivated by the hope of making money. So, when persecution came because of the Word, straightway he stumbled. Two of A-fa's relatives who were in the same trade, and after baptism had been employed as assistants in printing and book distribution, disappeared after release from prison. Another printer who had been arrested fled to Singapore when set at liberty, where he was employed by the American missionaries, and proved a useful and faithful worker.

By this time A-fa's son had returned to Canton, and was continuing his studies in Dr. Bridgman's home, where Dr. Medhurst met him. He says of him: "He has acquired a tolerable knowledge of the English language, while he pursues at the same time his Chinese studies. He is quiet, attentive, and obedient. Should he happily become the subject of serious impressions, and be endowed with a missionary spirit, he will be of much service to the Cause, and may one day prove a useful assistant in revising the Chinese version of the Scriptures. With this view Mr. Bridgman is already teaching him Hebrew, and will continue to afford him a thorough classical education. At present his situation is by no means comfortable, being confined entirely to the house, for should he appear on the streets his known connection with A-fa, and his own profession of Christianity, would expose him to immediate apprehension and punishment."[2] A-fa's wife and daughter had found temporary shelter with A-gong's wife—evidently now won over to sympathy—in his home near Whampoa. A-fa wished her to follow him to Singapore, but she was afraid of the sea voyage. From what he could learn Dr. Medhurst thought persecutions had combined with the instructions of her husband to enlighten her understanding and deepen in her heart an attachment to the Truth.

Dr. Medhurst later in the year became the unwitting cause of still further difficulty at Canton. He took a voyage with a Mr. Stevens, who had followed Abeel as seamen's chaplain, visiting various parts of four provinces and distributing a large quantity of literature. When news of this reached Peking a proclamation was issued denouncing his action and a commission was sent to Canton for the purpose of arresting the Chinese assisting foreigners to compose and print books. It was discovered that Dr. Bridgman had been connected with the work of printing, and the commission wished to make the Chinese security merchant who had guaranteed his bona fides when he arrived four years before responsible for his transgression of the law. The merchant cleared himself by proving that books were brought in from Malacca. A-teh was of course in imminent danger at Bridgman's house, and was sent secretly to Singapore. A-gong, who until then had been left in peace, was reported by an acquaintance whom he had unwittingly offended as being connected with missionaries, and a warrant was issued for his arrest. He was warned in time and fled to Lintin island, from whence he also proceeded in a British ship to Malacca. Here he joined his old companion A-fa in the work of the Mission. A-gong's son, who did not profess Christianity, was seized and forced to give information regarding the Chinese whom he knew to be connected with foreigners. After some months he was released, and earned at least the distinction of having his name mentioned in a Government edict. Just at this time—on Nov. 4, 1835—Dr. Peter Parker opened the ophthalmic hospital in the factory area at Canton. The activities of the Chinese authorities made it unwise for him to distribute any Christian literature or to do any preaching either public or private, which would have led to the closing of the institution, as the suspicious Government kept a constant watch on his movements.

For four years—until the end of 1839—Liang A-fa continued his work at Singapore and Malacca, paying only one brief visit to China in December 1836. When passing through Macao at this time he stayed with Mr. G. T. Lay, the first agent of the British and Foreign Bible Society in China. Mr. Lay says of him: "He spends most of his time reading the Scriptures with an anxious effort to understand them, but complains that though he can pray to the God of heaven he cannot find out the meaning of His Word. This is due in part to the natural compass and turn of the Chinese intellect, while English idiom and unintelligible phrases are every moment casting stumbling blocks in his way." During 1835 A-fa was associated with the Rev. Samuel Dyer who had been the inventor of movable Chinese metal type and was an earnest evangelist. The presence of both A-fa and A-gong at Malacca brought such a quickening to the work that 1837 was reported as the most successful year in the history of the Mission, with crowded attendances at the Chinese services. In the month of April twenty persons were admitted to the church by baptism. The following month ten more were received, one a venerable old man with a long white beard, who had been a teacher.

We are impressed by the liberal way in which these pioneers interpreted their task when we find A-fa assisting the Rev. I. Tracey of the American Board Mission to translate an address directed by the Singapore Agricultural and Horticultural Society to the Chinese farmers, and also composing a tract on "Incentives to abandon opium."[3] Social welfare effort of this kind has always been considered by the practical Chinese as a natural expression of Christ's ministry. The evangelist must have reveled in the freedom enjoyed for Christian work, which was in such marked contrast to the restrictions and persecution in the land from which he was banished for the Gospel's sake.

Nothing, however, could have induced Liang A-fa to work permanently outside China. He had heard a call to preach the Gospel to his own people, and not even the fruitful harvest among Chinese emigrants could satisfy his heart. Towards the close of 1839 he returned to Canton. Since Dr. Morrison's death over five years before, no British missionary had been stationed there. Fortunately a few American missionaries had been able to remain, although their work was difficult owing to political unrest, and bore little direct fruit. The British Government had taken no further steps to enforce the demands presented through Lord Napier. His nation was still considered a tribe of merchant barbarians under tribute to the Emperor of China. After the ambassador left Canton on account of serious illness from which he died at Macao, trade relations were resumed under the old vexatious and humiliating conditions. The position was so intolerable that an open rupture was only a question of tune.

The immediate occasion was finally found in connection with the traffic in opium. During 1838 Emperor Tao Kwang, in response to numerous memorials petitioning him to prevent the open smuggling of the drug in foreign ships of various nationalities, and under the protection of his own conniving officials, decided on drastic action. He appointed Lin Tse-su, then Viceroy of Hupeh and Hunan, to represent the Throne in a final settlement of the matter. Commissioner Lin arrived at Canton on March

10, 1839. Eight days later he commanded that all opium on foreign ships and in warehouses should be immediately handed over to the Chinese authorities, and that foreigners should be under bond never again to import the drug. When the British did not at once comply with this order the factory area was surrounded by soldiers, and no foreigners were allowed to leave the city. The next step was to call out the several hundred Chinese in foreign employment. Lin also threatened the foreign community with mob attack if they did not yield. Under such extreme pressure the British had no option, and by May 21 the whole stock of opium in foreign hands—20,283 chests valued at two million pounds sterling—had been delivered to the Commissioner. This was completely destroyed. Thus was precipitated the first war between Britain and China, lasting from September 1839 until August 1842.

Most fair-minded people today, Chinese and Western, would admit the truth of the following statement made by an American historian:— "The first war with China was but the beginning of a struggle between the extreme East and the West; the East refusing to treat on terms of equality—diplomatically and commercially—with Western nations, and the West insisting on its right to be so treated."[4] It must be frankly confessed however, and was so by leading British statesmen at the time, that their nation's participation in a traffic which was destroying millions of people body and soul was a shameful crime. True the East India Company had ceased to carry opium on their ships after the interdiction of the trade by the Chinese Government in 1800, but British India was the main source of supply, and the bulk of it was smuggled in British ships. Revenue was placed before righteousness.

Liang A-fa arrived at Canton just before the outbreak of war. The prospect filled him with dismay, and caused him acute distress. In his patriotic earnestness and Christian zeal he felt something must be done to prevent it. He made his way to the foreign factories and called on John R. Morrison, then representing the British Government in Canton, and entreated him to use his influence for the preservation of peace. The argument advanced by the evangelist was characteristic. He said he feared if the British came to fight with the Chinese, his countrymen would never afterwards receive the Scriptures, nor listen to the preaching of the Gospel by British missionaries. The interests of Christianity should therefore weigh with the British Government and should induce Mr. Morrison to exhaust every means in trying to prevent hostilities. Young Morrison must have been deeply moved by this appeal made by his father's old friend. It was too late to avert the coming crash, and at any rate it was beyond the power of either Morrison or A-fa. But, familiar with the natural timidity of the Chinese, we must admire the courage of this man who dared to visit the representative of the enemy Government when his own past history and the present situation made his action so hazardous. The only motive which inspired such disregard for his own safety was anxiety for the coming of Christ's Kingdom in China.

Even so it is somewhat surprising to find A-fa carrying on evangelistic work in Canton, evidently without interference by the Government. One reason may have been that the officials were too busy with weightier matters to concern themselves with him. Again they might hesitate to antagonize the American community by arresting one who was so highly esteemed by some of its business as well as missionary members. There was still another reason, however, and this, while not minimizing our estimate of the courage shown by A-fa, may explain why he was allowed access to the factory area at all at such a time. Shortly after Commissioner Lin arrived in Canton he found it necessary to engage an interpreter who understood the English language. Hearing of A-fa's son, A-teh, then twenty years of age, he offered him an appointment on his staff. So this young man, trained for eight years in the home of Dr. Bridgman with a view to fitting him for Christian work, became the Commissioner's English translator. Under such circumstances the father was much less likely to be interfered with, and his former transgression of the law would be conveniently forgotten, at any rate while the Commissioner employing the son was in control. It gives an added interest to this unfortunate chapter in Anglo-Chinese history to find the sons of Dr. Morrison and Liang A-fa playing such parts in it.

Early in the war the Rev. Wm. C. Milne, son of Dr. William Milne, arrived at Macao, ready to take up the work his father and Dr. Morrison had laid down. He was accompanied by Dr. B. Hobson. Unable to visit Canton on account of hostilities, and knowing it would be extremely dangerous for A-fa to attempt a trip to Macao, he sent him a letter under cover to Dr. Parker. He received a very touching epistle in reply, wherein the evangelist recalled standing at the foot of the steps outside the door of the Anglo-Chinese College at Malacca watching Dr. Milne's four children embarking on a ship for England after the death of their parents. The younger boy suddenly refused to go on the boat, and turned back crying towards the College. A-fa was so grieved by the sight that he retired to his room and wept. Many times he had prayed they might be guarded and blessed. Now the news that the eldest son (one of the twins born on shipboard when the parents and A-fa had first sailed from Macao in 1815) had succeeded to his father's pastoral office, and come to China to continue his work, filled his heart with joy and gratitude. Since A-fa's return from Malacca he had already baptized four persons, and a regular congregation of twelve believers met under his leadership to worship. A-fa would be thinking of his hopes for his own boy as he wrote this welcome to the son of his spiritual father.

The evangelist had now made his permanent home in Canton. His fellow clansmen at Lohtsun Village had suffered so much through imprisonment, fines, and loss of property when the soldiers made their unsuccessful attempt to arrest A-fa in 1834, that they were naturally averse to his return. They had no desire to run a similar risk again. And they held A-fa responsible to refund what they had lost, which was rather a formidable demand. A-fa recognized the justice of their claims and did what he could to make restitution, but at his death he still had not entirely satisfied them. One of the hindrances to Christian work in that region today is the tradition that he and his family have never yet cleared up this matter to the satisfaction of the clan. In recording the loss of his ancestral heritage and the enmity of his own folk he uses the words of St. Paul "Far be it from me to glory, save in the cross of our Lord Jesus Christ, through which the world hath been crucified unto me and I unto the world." He secured a residence in Lung Mei To (The Way of the Dragon's Tail). Village at Honam, on the opposite side of the river from Canton city. While the city was being attacked in 1841 some cannon balls fell near his house, but no one was hurt.

The evangelist found a welcome opportunity in Dr. Parker's hospital, which he often visited to talk with the patients. He said "When I meet men in the streets and villages and tell them of the folly of worshipping idols they laugh at me. Their hearts are very hard. But when men are sick and are healed their hearts are very soft." Dr. Parker quoted this statement when speaking before the Senate and House of Representatives at Washington U.S.A. on Sunday, January 31, 1841, and added "Of the hospital he might speak feelingly, for he had been successfully treated for a disease which in the hands of a native practitioner often proves fatal. Had I accomplished no other good than being instrumental in restoring to health this deal servant of God my mission had not been in vain." Here we have one of the reasons why Dr. Parker can be said to have "opened China with the point of the lancet."

Commissioner Lin was removed from his special office (although retained as Viceroy of the two Kwang provinces) in 1840, and Kishen succeeded him, A-teh was urged by his father and friends not to accept reappointment on the yamen staff. The young man went to Macao, where he visited Dr. Hobson, who makes the following comment on his visitor: "During this, his first experience of public life, his Christian principles appear to have abided by him, and time only can show how much influence his translations and his knowledge of foreigners has had upon the counsels of Peking. We are inclined to think it has been great." It was the first time in history that the foreign point of view had been placed before the Chinese Imperial Court. A large part of A-teh's work had been to translate extracts from the English papers published in Macao. These were forwarded by the Commissioner to Peking, and came before the attention of the Emperor and his advisors. A-teh had been recently married, and Dr. Bridgman, along with Mr. Morrison, became responsible for the support of the young couple while A-teh continued his Chinese studies. The father thought that after ten more years of such study his son might be equipped for the task of Bible translation.

A-fa rejoiced greatly when the cessation of fighting allowed him to visit his missionary friends at Macao in September 1841. In each home the servants were gathered, and the evangelist read and explained the Scriptures to them. He gave to the missionaries a list of the corrections he had been making in Dr. Medhurst's version of the New Testament. One of his activities which interested his friends was the teaching of his daughter A-chim to read. This must have been a rare accomplishment for a girl of her station in these days. Speaking of his lonely position and difficult work at Canton during the absence of the missionaries and amid war conditions he said "I must sow the seed and (pointing to heaven) the God of heaven will send the showers."

Illustration 11.1 Samchow Market.

Illustration 11.2 Liang A-fa's House on Honam, Canton.

Illustration 11.3 Liang A-fa Memorial Centre at Samchow Temporary Quarters opened 1933.

Illustration 11.4 Grave of Liang A-fa in centre of Lingnan University Campus.

Notes

1. Edith Cavell (1865–1915) was a nurse during World War I who helped Allied soldiers escape from Belgium and was subsequently executed. MacLennan was assistant conference secretary at the World Missionary Conference in Edinburgh 1910 and a leader in the missionary movement.

2. Medhurst, *China: Its State and Prospects, with Especial Reference to the Spread of the Gospel; Containing Allusions to the Antiquity, Extent, Population, Civilization, Literature, and Religion of the Chinese* (Boston: Crocker & Brewster, 1838), 298–99.

3. Wylie notes Liang's assistance to Tracey with two anti-opium tracts.

4. Francis Lister Hawks Pott, *The Emergency in China* (New York: Missionary Education Movement of the United States and Canada, 1913), 14.

12

God's Things and Caesar's

"For the past century and more, the same intense international and interracial struggle which at once developed and devastated Europe has unfortunately been finding its way to the Far East. Because of this, Chinese patriotic feeling has been gradually taking on a new complexion. We can hardly criticize the Chinese people as being too nationalistic or narrowly patriotic when they try to resist the inroads of foreign influences, the imperialistic designs of the foreign Powers, and the inequalities imposed on China by sheer force."

—Dr. David Z. T. Yui[1]

Under the terms of peace at the conclusion of the first war between Britain and China, Canton, (along with Amoy, Foochow, Ningpo, and Shanghai) became open ports for foreign residence and trade, and the island of Hong Kong—just outside the mouth of the Canton River—was ceded to Britain. This island had been used by the British during the war, as it provided a convenient harbor for their ships. While the treaty of Nanking did not immediately remove restrictions on missionary work and allow religious freedom, it did provide the missionary societies with a new and safe base of operations in closest proximity to China. True, Britain had little to be proud of in the method of occupation. But she did only what almost any other Power would have done at that date given a like reason and a similar opportunity. The churches both in Europe and America doubtless felt it was a providential happening.

The London Missionary Society transferred its headquarters from Malacca to Hong Kong. Other societies followed suit. Dr. J. Ledge, then

principal of the Anglo-Chinese College, brought with him several helpers. The most outstanding was a young man named Ho Tsun-shin, the son
of a printer who had formerly worked with Liang A-fa. Ho had received
a thorough Chinese classical education before entering College. He made
such progress under Dr. Legge's tuition that he could read both the Old and
New Testaments fluently in the original, and could actually compose in
Hebrew. He became also a most earnest and eloquent preacher Dr. Legge
said he had never heard a better preacher anywhere. One evening he was
speaking in a crowded church, many of the audience having to stand, on
the story of Job. When he described Job taking a potsherd to scrape himself,
he stooped down as if to pick one up. Dr. Legge, standing in the crowd,
came to himself by finding his own hands on the tile floor. Looking around
he saw that scores in the audience were bent double in imitation of the
preacher, completely carried away by his eloquence and dramatic power.
After a few years of service Mr. Ho was ordained to the pastorate of the
first Chinese congregation in Hong Kong on Sunday, October 11, 1846.
Although repeatedly offered five times his salary as a preacher to enter mer-
cantile or government service, he remained with the mission until his death
in 1870. One of his daughters still lives—Madame Wu Ting-fang. For some
months during 1843 and 1844 Liang A-fa and Ho Tsun-shin were associated in evangelistic work at Hong Kong, and opened a number of preaching
centers. Kew A-gong had also accompanied Dr. Legge, and was likewise
engaged in preaching. Unfortunately a quarrel arose between A-gong and
A-fa. Owing to this estrangement and also because of his father's serious
illness A-fa returned to Canton. The father died on February 20, 1844, at
the ripe age of eighty-seven.

A-teh had also been employed in mission work at the new centre, perhaps assisting Dr. Legge in the school, but his experiences were not at all
happy. He considered the Colony a low place—the resort of the worst class
of Chinese, driven thither by destitution or crime. On return to Canton
he entered the employment of Powtinqua, the principal Chinese merchant
engaged in foreign trade, as English interpreter. He never afterwards took
part in mission work. For this reason the missionaries looked on him with
suspicion and disappointment as one who had been tempted by material
advantages. While in the employment of this firm he was repeatedly invited into the presence of Ke-ying, Viceroy and High Commissioner, who
consulted him regarding the customs, history, and power of the different
European nations. The Commissioner used the knowledge thus obtained

in memorializing the Emperor. In 1845 he wrote: "Last year I was commissioned to go to Liang Kwang (Kwangtung and Kwangsi) and also received the Emperor's command to tranquillize the affairs of the foreigners. I therefore made direct enquiry concerning the religion practiced by Western men in order to ascertain whether it was corrupt or pure. Having carefully examined all the time I was there, I came to know that what they taught had really nothing in it which was not good. I felt therefore that I ought to memorialize the Emperor, and request that, showing kindness to men from afar, he would not persecute or prohibit it."[2] Ke-ying was a Manchu whose previous appointments in Manchuria and Peking had already brought him into slight contact with foreigners. As one of the Chinese plenipotentiaries signing the treaty of Nanking he had come into closer touch with the representatives of other nations. While in Canton he had been treated medically by Dr. Parker. Between sixty and seventy years of age, he was a stout, hale, good-humored old gentleman with a firm step and upright carriage. Imagination can draw a fascinating picture of the Manchu courtier in intimate conversation with the young Cantonese whose circumstances had given him such a favored opportunity of appreciating foreign friends, and especially their Christian beliefs.

Ke-ying, in the essay quoted above, relates the experience of his private secretary, who when sick had sought relief in vain from the gods, doctors, and diviners, but who, hearing how foreigners prayed to God, had prayed in like manner and had immediately been healed. Afterwards he had always found prayer efficacious when in difficulty. The secretary asked Ke-ying to prepare a prayer for him, and a most reverent and beautifully-worded prayer is included in the essay. It reminds one of those wonderful prayers to Heaven which are recorded in the Chinese classical books, and the conviction deepens that it is in prayer the very heart of true religion is found. The ancient Temple of Heaven at Peking and its worship was not so far in spirit from the temple at Jerusalem. "God is no respecter of persons: but in every nation he that feareth him and worketh righteousness is acceptable to him."[3]

The British Government and the foreign community at Canton suffered a sad loss when Mr. John R. Morrison died in August 1843, not yet thirty years of age. He had carried heavy responsibility through these anxious months, specially during the peace negotiations, when he acted as secretary to Sir Henry Pottinger, the British Ambassador. But he was missed just as much by his Chinese friends. Liang A-fa was greatly moved by his early death. He recalled the help received from him in his own trouble, and, reflecting on the brevity of life, decided he must buy up every opportunity to preach the Gospel. A-fa himself had been far from well. In a letter to the Society he writes of his many ailments, and the difficulty of carrying on in enfeebled health. While he could not move about so freely he still gathered the believers in his home, preached the Good News to visitors, and used his enforced inactivity to revise his tracts and books, and to prepare a list of suggested amendments to the translation of the Bible.

When the terms of the Nanking treaty were known abroad the attention of other Governments was immediately directed to their relations with China. It was evident the privileges of residence and trade granted to Britain could not be withheld from other Powers. The supplementary treaty of the Bogue signed about two years later by the representatives of Britain and China made this point perfectly clear, and contained the "most-favored-nation" clause, incorporated afterwards in all treaties of the various Governments with China. This clause claimed for all the privileges granted to any. The United States sent the Hon. Caleb Cushing to negotiate a treaty. Dr. Bridgman and Dr. Parker were appointed joint secretaries in Chinese to the special commission, and a treaty was signed at Wanghia, near Macao, on July 3, 1844. Ke-ying represented China, and it is quite likely A-teh was present as an assistant, although he took no official part. In a letter dated May 6 of that year, A-fa says his son is going to accompany Mr. Cushing to help in organizing a friendly understanding between the two countries. This treaty was the first to provide for the founding of Christian churches and hospitals in the open ports.

The following year toleration was officially granted to Christianity (Roman Catholic and Protestant) throughout the whole Empire. This was, as already indicated, in response to representations made by Ke-ying, and primarily at the request of the French Ambassador. The religious liberty now provided for in the constitution of the Chinese Republic has made these toleration clauses in the old treaties obsolete. They are not only useless but harmful. While neither China nor the Powers pay any regard to them they are still part of the so-called "unequal treaties" and as such obnoxious to patriotic Chinese Christians. They are quite out of harmony with the present state of autonomy enjoyed by the churches in China. Providing a ready excuse for anti-Christian attack and material for propaganda the sooner they are scrapped the better. It must not be forgotten, however, that the situation was very different when these treaties were first signed. Until these clauses were agreed to it was a crime punishable by death for either foreigners or Chinese to preach Christ in China. The unfortunate thing— though seemingly inevitable—was that provisions granting freedom to the Christian religion should have been mixed up with humiliating treaties forced upon an unwilling China by war. Liang A-fa and his son were not very optimistic when they heard of their new liberty. A-teh expressed the opinion that officials in the interior would defeat the purpose of the treaty by making it impossible for the missionaries to secure land or by some other device.

The Church Missionary Society sent a deputation in 1844 to visit the new treaty ports with a view to opening work. One of the deputies was the Rev. George Smith who afterwards (in 1850) became the first Bishop of Victoria, Hong Kong. When they arrived at Canton, Mr. Smith wished to make arrangements for temporary residence outside the factory area, and the abbot of the Honam Buddhist monastery met him at Dr. Parker's house to discuss possibilities of his staying at the temple and studying Mandarin there. While they were talking together another visitor arrived. We shall let Mr. Smith describe the meeting: "Before the abbot's departure we had a visit from an individual well-known by name in Europe and America as the first fruits of modern Protestant missionary effort among the Chinese, and the first native evangelist to his fellow-countrymen—Liang A-fa. He appeared about sixty years of age; a man of sturdy dimensions, of cheerful manners and a venerable aspect. He seemed greatly interested in our arrival, and joined with much animation in the conversation. The sight of such a trophy of the converting power of God's grace excited emotions of joy in our minds such as can only be estimated by those placed in a similar position. It refreshed the weary eye as the fair green oasis in the desert. We were a somewhat remarkable assemblage. On the one hand was a native scholar, accounted wise and honorable, and yet the slave of a debasing idolatry, ignorant of the true God and of Jesus Christ the Savior of mankind. On the other hand sat a Chinese, less deeply versed perhaps in the vagaries of pagan learning, but taught by the Spirit of God, and rescued from sin and death by Divine grace—the wisdom of the world and the wisdom of God. I was pleased to observe that neither Liang A-fa nor the priest showed any marks of an uncourteous disposition. They exchanged the usual signs of salutation, and conversed with apparent affability. The Christian meekness of the one and the true native politeness of the other prevented the indication of anything like illiberal antipathy."[4]

Mr. Smith was the guest of Dr. and Mrs. Peter Parker. His hostess was the first foreign woman to reside for any time in the factory area at Canton. On Sunday morning, October 13, 1844, Mr. Smith preached to about forty Europeans and Americans in Dr. Parker's dining room. During the afternoon Dr. and Mrs. Parker, Liang A-fa, Rev. T. M. McClatchie (another member of the C.M.S. deputation) and Mr. Smith joined in partaking of the Lord's Supper. Mr. Smith writes: "An unusual solemnity pervaded the occasion, and we felt the privilege of Christian communion with each other at this distance from the churches of our respective fatherlands. We assembled few in number, fewer than the original apostles—and, like them, in an upper room, with a world lying around in unbelief. There we penitentially confessed our sinfulness and implored strength for our work. There we anew commemorated that Savior's death on Whom we built our hopes of acceptance, and in obedience to Whose command 'Go and teach all nations' we had come hither. And even here we were not without encouragement in the fact of our approaching the Lord's table with one, who, himself the first fruits of modern missionary effort in China, was now an evangelist to his own countrymen. We sang some hymns appropriate to our situation, and the service was concluded by Liang A-fa praying in Chinese for the spread of the Gospel and the conversion of his country. The earnestness of his tone plainly told us the fervency of his intercessions on this occasion were indeed ardent."[5] Thus the first Bishop of Victoria was consecrated by the prayer of Liang A-fa some years before being set apart in Canterbury Cathedral for his work in China.

Ten days later, A-fa brought his son to meet Mr. Smith. A-teh was very critical of the English attitude towards the Chinese, specially as evidenced in the ill treatment of his countrymen by the police of Hong Kong and during the recent war. He said until they showed a kinder spirit, Christianity would never be respected. The war had made the Chinese less inclined to listen to the Gospel than formerly. The father evinced a more meek and gentle spirit. When Mr. Smith expressed the hope that he might win many souls he said with much feeling "If foreign Christians have such love for souls as to come to preach the Gospel to the Chinese who hate them, how much more ought I, a Chinese, to exert myself for the conversion of my countrymen."[6] When asked what were the chief hindrances he said the greatest was hardness of heart, which only God could soften. Mr. Smith told the old man how many Christians in England took an affectionate interest in his work. This assurance moved him to tears. Raising his hand to heaven he said he prayed with all his heart he might become what he should be.

Notes

1. This is David. Z. T. Yui (Yu Rizhang, 1882–1936), who was a YMCA official. See Daniel Bays, "Yu, David Z. T.," 757, in Gerald Anderson, ed., *Biographical Dictionary of Christian Missions* (New York: Simon & Schuster Macmillan, 1998).

2. *The Chinese Repository, Volume 15* (Canton, Jan. 1851), 43.

3. This is a direct quote of Acts 10:34 (KJV).

4. G. Smith, *A Narrative of an Exploratory Visit to Each of the Consular Cities of China and to the Islands of Hong Kong and Chusan in Behalf of the Church Missionary Society in the Years 1844, 1845, 1846, Second Edition* (London: Seeley, Burnside, & Seeley, 1847), 10–11.

5. Ibid., 38.

6. Ibid., 54.

13

Go—Preach—Heal

"How can I leave these dear and precious souls for whom there are so few to care? Help us to maintain the combat in this great heathen city until its gates are opened to the King of Glory! Brethren, pray for us that the word of the Lord may have free course and be glorified." At Canton in 1850.

—Rev. W. M. C. Burns[1]

After he had spent some months in Canton the Mission proposed that Liang A-fa should return to preach in Hong Kong, and Dr. Legge arranged suitable quarters for him. But he excused himself on account of his many ailments and increasing weakness; also on the ground of anxiety over his wife who was in feeble health. He said the climate of Hong Kong did not agree with him, and he felt unhappy there because of an unfortunate experience when some Englishman—perhaps intoxicated—tried to ride him down. There was something else, however, which troubled his conscience, prejudiced him against residence in Hong Kong, and for the time affected his usefulness and the work of the Mission. This was his estrangement from his companion of many years—Kew A-gong. At last he yielded to the pressure of his friends and resumed his labors in Hong Kong, preaching with much acceptance.

In January of 1845 the members of the London Missionary Society met in Hong Kong to celebrate the jubilee of the Society by a day of prayer. With the missionaries were gathered four Chinese helpers. Dr. Legge writes: "Our engagements were preceded by an auspicious circumstance. Kew A-gong and Liang A-fa consented to bury their animosities and gave each other the right hand of fellowship, exchanging the salutation of brethren. We believe that the root of bitterness has thus been extirpated from our small circle, and are more prepared to pray for and expect the Divine blessing to rest upon our Mission." None of the missionaries knew what had caused the enmity between the two old friends. There was great joy when the Paul and Barnabas of South China, who had hazarded their lives for the name of the Lord Jesus Christ, were reconciled.

However important and successful the work in Hong Kong might be, the Mission felt its responsibility for the evangelization of the populous city of Canton. In fact plans were already being prepared for beginning work in all the treaty ports. In July of that year the Rev. Wm. Gillespie and A-fa rented a house at San Sha, a street in the southern suburbs of Canton near the river shore. For three of four months after opening the chapel the neighbors were quiet and peaceful. But just then Dr. Legge became ill and had to sail for England. Mr. Gillespie was forced to take over his duties in Hong Kong. The people of the neighborhood turned suspicious, and stories were spread around that A-fa had been sent by the British Government to buy the hearts of the Chinese people so that the land might be conquered. The chapel and preacher were said to represent a continuation of the enemy's attack, using new and more subtle methods. Considering the evangelist a traitor, a mob attacked the place and smashed up the furniture, carrying away some of the things. A-fa's life was in grave danger, but he managed to escape. The owner of the house was threatened with punishment if he continued to rent it to foreigners. Thus the first attempt to secure a footing in the city failed.

A-fa found another sphere of service, however, and one very much after his own heart, as well as being secure from molestation. His interest in Dr. Parker's hospital has already been mentioned. He was invited to become hospital evangelist, and began his new duties on December 29, 1845. This hospital was the pioneer of its kind in the Far East, being founded in November 1835. It was at first known as the Ophthalmic Hospital, as its primary purpose was to afford relief to the many suffering from affections of the eyes. But so many came seeking healing for other complaints that restriction to one class of disease became impossible. The founder was Dr. Peter Parker of the American Board Mission. The hospital was situated in the factory area, in a house opening on the dirty crowded thoroughfare fittingly known as Hog Lane. In such insanitary surroundings, and with the most meager equipment, the skill and kindness of the missionary surgeon speedily attracted crowds of both rich and poor seeking relief from suffering. This institution, under the name of the Canton Hospital, has continued its gracious ministry until the present day, and is thus just completing its first century. In its earliest years it was thought unwise to make any attempt at public preaching or to use Christian literature. The work of the doctor, his character, and the quiet word he was able to drop into the minds of grateful patients or their friends, were eloquent enough. With the increasing prestige of the institution, however, and specially after the signing of the treaties with Britain and America, it became possible to carry on regular Christian services in the hospital. At Liang A-fa's first Sunday service there were about eighty Chinese present and two missionaries. The following Sunday one hundred and eighty gathered, and on the third about two hundred. Thus A-fa felt that a great door and effectual had been opened for the Gospel through the hospital. From the record of attendances he kept the evangelist reckoned upwards of fifteen thousand persons heard the Gospel during the first three and a half years. A-fa mourned that out of all this multitude only three were interested enough to really study the Truth, and even of these not one was ready for baptism. Quite evidently the soil of Cantonese hearts was hard indeed when the softening influences of the hospital were not enough to make them responsive to such a message.

That the seeming failure was not due to lack of earnestness or ability in the preacher we know from what Dr. Parker writes of him: "His preaching is characterized by great sincerity and often pathos. With much humility he frequently tells his audience that he has been a servant of the Gospel for thirty years, and understands it a little. With great force he informs them that he was once an idolater, and was as strong in his prejudice against Christianity as others, and equally skeptical as to the life after death. But he says that was because of his ignorance of the Gospel. Heavenly light had not then illumined his dark mind. His prayers are most fervent, and his Christian views strongly evangelical. His illustrations of the Scriptures are clear, and his appeals frequently powerful in their impression upon his auditors." In a later report Dr. Parker says: "With happy effect he dwelt upon the Savior's life and example, and pointing to the paintings and illustrations of cures suspended on the walls of the room, informed his auditors that these were performed by His blessing and in conformity to His precepts and example."[2] The paintings referred to were portraits of a large number of Dr. Parker's patients, showing their ailments, and their appearance after being cured. These were the work of an artist named Lamqua, and were presented to the doctor soon after the opening of the hospital. A medical visitor from England in 1836 says of them: "Whether it is to be attributed to the skill of the native limners who execute these works of art I will not pretend to decide, but certainly many of these men and women appear as good looking before as after the operation, notwithstanding the enormous tumors and awkward blemishes which have been removed." Some of the portraits were later taken to England by Dr. Parker, and may still be seen in the Gordon Museum of Guy's Hospital in London. In addition to taking the Sun-day services A-fa was also in attendance every Monday morning, when he addressed the crowds gathered for treatment.

Perhaps helped by his son, who had of course a much larger salary than the father, A-fa built a new house in the village on Honam in 1846. The name of the village, meaning "The Way of the Dragon's Tail" probably had reference to the propitious geomantic influences supposed to emanate from the geographical configuration of the surrounding country, and controlled by two high pagodas on Honam Island. The site of the house was at the base of a low hill covered with graves, where ordinary Chinese, with their traditional fear of demons, would have been afraid to live. Attached to the house he erected a hall which could seat about a hundred persons. This place was dedicated for public worship in a service held on October 18. The Lord's Supper was administered to a small group of eight persons, two of whom had just recently been baptized. The furniture and inscriptions on the walls were such as had been salvaged from the riot at the former chapel in the city, but the building was put up by the evangelist at his own expense. Every Sunday he conducted a service here before crossing the river to the hospital. This church in his house met there regularly until his death, and daily prayers were held. The house still stands, and is occupied by a non-Christian relative. The tablets and images of the idol shrine are sadly out of harmony with the memories and feelings that stir the Christian visitor.

The anti-foreign feeling following the war becoming less virulent, Dr. Hobson, who had recently returned from furlough, came to Canton seeking an opening for medical work. He brought with him as his wife Dr. Morrison's eldest daughter. He first rented part of a house occupied by an American missionary, while Liang A-fa searched the city and Honam for an available centre. At last he found an old empty warehouse on the river front in a place called Kam-li-fau. This was rented and altered to serve as a consulting room and dispensary. In the beginning of April 1848 medical work was commenced. Every Monday, Wednesday, and Friday patients came to see the doctor, and A-fa was present to tell them of the Great Physician. The first day only four patients came, but on the second there were upwards of twenty, and after that the doors were never opened on dispensary day without admitting more than a hundred people. Undoubtedly the good work done by Dr. Parker in his hospital during the twelve years had proved an excellent advertisement for Western medicine and surgery. Finding the experiment so successful Dr. Hobson had the whole building transformed into a dwelling house, chapel, and hospital, and moved into the premises with his family. From the opening day until the call came to lay down his task Liang A-fa was the faithful evangelist in the "Hospital of Merciful Love," as it was called in Chinese. He had naturally to relinquish his duties in Dr. Parker's institution. Fittingly on the first Sunday after the building was occupied the little Chinese Church gathered in the chapel to celebrate the Lord's Supper, four men and six women communicating. Pastor Liang conducted the service.

The following Sunday public preaching services were commenced, when the pastor addressed two hundred and thirty people. It was rather a difficult audience. The people went out and came in, greeting their acquaintances in the accustomed hearty manner, talking and laughing about this strange kind of worship without visible gods, robed priests, altar, incense, or sacrifice. Many however were attentive, listening with evident approval. Throughout the summer of 1848 the average number of patients was two hundred and fifty per day. At 9:30 each morning A-fa addressed the sick folk and their friends, and a tract with a Scripture message and a simple form of prayer was given to each. While the doctor was busy in the consulting room the evangelist was as busy in the waiting hall. Dr. Hobson, writing of their experience during these strenuous but happy opening months, said: "Dear old Liang A-fa gives me great satisfaction. He preaches the Gospel faithfully, affectionately, and in the most intelligent and earnest manner. He told me the other day that he had never felt such interest in the work as he has done since the hospital was opened. He is listened to with great attention, and feels deeply the subject he preaches to others. In fulfilling his duty he is watered himself, and is rejoicing in hope of the Kingdom of God. His prayers are the earnest breathing of a Christian heart. It is grateful to one's ear as well as to one's soul to listen to and join in them when so fervently and devoutly presented at the Throne of Grace."

The foregoing is a very heartening testimony. The combination of affection, intelligence, and earnestness in the preacher, the fact that he shared the experience of Bunyan "I preached what I felt, what I smartingly did feel," and the sincerity and directness of his prayers as well as of his preaching are marks of a competent evangelist. Faithfulness does not, however, ensure a continuance of success. Next year the average number of patients dropped to one hundred and fifty a day. The doctor, diagnosed the reason in the disinclination of many to listen to the foreign doctrine. Rather than be forced to hear it they would take their chances of healing elsewhere. "Are not Abanah and Pharpar, the rivers of Damascus, better than all the waters of Israel?"[3] China had her own sages, and the humbling truths of the Gospel were distasteful to them. The preacher's experience was that when he taught the duty of the people of all nations worshipping the one true God many accepted it, but when he went on to say they must trust in Jesus Christ for salvation from sin they rejected the message. The increasing unresponsiveness of his fellow-countrymen to the Gospel was a sore grief to the evangelist. It was only rarely that he was really disheartened. Dr. Hobson thus describes one of his black days: "Liang A-fa was out of spirits this morning, and said he had no heart to preach to the sick people. I took him aside and enquired the cause of his depression. He said his wife was sick, that the Chinese were very wicked, that the Christians were not as united as they ought to be, and so on. I spoke to him of how much the foreign missionaries had to bear from the Chinese, and yet they persisted in their work. If such were the feelings, wishes, and principles of foreigners, surely a Chinese preacher, especially an experienced man like the evangelist, should not lose heart in urging his countrymen to abandon their idols and worship the true God. Then I reminded him how much provocation, insult and contempt Jesus our Savior patiently endured. This conversation had a good effect. The old man was nerved to renewed effort, and spoke better and more earnestly to the patients than I remember to have heard him before."

The partnership between Dr. Hobson and Liang A-fa was very intimate. The evangelist described the doctor as a man with a fervent, sincere, affectionate and benevolent heart, who day and night gave himself for others. When he compared himself with his medical brother he felt himself unworthy to be called a follower of Jesus. Dr. Hobson's knowledge of the Scriptures was a great help to him, and he was able to suggest many new plans for the work which the evangelist eagerly welcomed. But the medical missionary felt it was right [that] the main responsibility for the evangelistic and pastoral work should rest on his Chinese colleague, who had been set apart to that office.

An interesting instance of the far-reaching results of this cooperation and also of the united influence of evangelistic, medical, and literary work is worth recording. A Christian named Loh was employed as a gatekeeper at the hospital. In his spare time he carried a bag of Christian books and tracts into the city, and distributed them as he found opportunity. Loh had a friend—in a certain shop, and so he went there with his tracts. He gave a copy of Dr. Milne's tract "The Conversation of Two Friends" to a Mr. Chau, who was living in the same place. Mr. Chau had been familiar with Chinese classical literature from his childhood, but this little book made an appeal to his heart that nothing else he had read had ever done. The young scholar—he was twenty-four years old—was persuaded to attend the Sunday service in the hospital chapel. He was surprised and touched by the warm welcome he received from the foreign doctor and his wife. The earnest preaching of old Pastor Liang moved him deeply. For a whole year he went regularly to church, and also studied the Scriptures under the guidance of his new friends. Then, on a Sunday he would never forget, the pastor baptized him into the fellowship that had become his spiritual home. Some time later Dr. Hobson was translating a text-book on "Physiology" into Chinese, and wished to have it illustrated with diagrams and drawings. He asked Mr. Chau to help him. The care and excellence with which he did this work still further attracted the doctor to him, and he was engaged as assistant to Pastor Liang. He began by giving short talks at the Sunday services after the pastor had preached, and in this practical way he was trained for evangelistic work. His help became more and more valuable as he grew in Christian experience and knowledge and became increasingly efficient in public address and personal persuasion. Thus, as Pastor Liang was gradually forced by increasing infirmity and the frailty of old age to reduce his activities, the young helper was able to take over the burden. After A-fa's death Mr. Chau continued to preach in the hospital chapel, and carried on until the institution was closed when war broke out again between Britain and China. Dr. Hobson did not vacate his charge until the cannon balls began to hurtle over the city. Later Mr. Chau joined the Rev. George Piercy, (pioneer missionary of the English Wesleyan Mission), at Macao, returning with him to Canton when peace was declared. For the long period of forty-five years Mr. Chau was associated with that Society as preacher, pastor, and teacher. Latterly he was set apart to the training of catechists. Some years before his death this fine old veteran affirmed his conviction that nothing could happen which would successfully interfere with the progress of the Gospel of Jesus Christ in China. Looking back over the marvelous development that had marked his own life-time he died in the faith that the day was hastening when his countrymen throughout the whole land would bow at the feet of Jesus. Thus through all the men, women and children whose lives Pastor Chau touched in Christ's Name, and through all the preachers whom he trained, and again through the many more whom they in turn have won to the Savior, Liang A-fa lives on. "God buries His workmen but carries on His work."

Notes

1. Wylie describes a William Burns who published a dozen works in Chinese as well as a volume in English. This is probably the English Presbyterian Missionary William Chalmers Burns (1815–1868).

2. Eighty of the paintings commissioned by Peter Parker are archived by Yale. They were created by Lam Qua, a painter who studied with George Chinnery in the 1820s.

3. 2 Kings 5:12 (American Standard Version).

14

The Last Crossing

"There is one chapter in the biography of a great genius, an eminent saint
or seer, which has for us generally special interest, into which we are most
curious to dip—the chapter entitled 'Closing Days'—curious to learn how he
bore himself, or what fell from his lips during those days in the shadow of the
approaching end."

S. A. TIPPLE[1]

Liang A-fa's wife died in 1849. He had been very anxious about her for
some time. Dr. Hobson speaks of her early that year as "a quiet good
woman in feeble health." During a long partnership, tested by the many
dangers through which her husband passed, and long separations for
the Gospel's sake, with the constant scorn and of relatives and neighbors
because of her Christian profession, she remained loyal to her husband
and true to her Savior. It is surely a testimony to her earnestness that her
old mother and widowed sister had become Christians and lived in the
home. The daughter-in-law, also a church member, with her young children, formed part of the household. A-teh had gone with Dr. Bridgman to
Shanghai, and was probably not with his mother when she died.

His relatives, anxious that the old man should have proper care, persuaded him to marry again some months later. Unfortunately the woman
became dissatisfied and left him, marrying elsewhere. Another wife was
then arranged for who survived him. This trouble in his home was not only
a grief to A-fa, but was an anxiety to his Christian friends. While the second
marriage was perfectly legal, and the plans of the relatives well meant, no

regular Christian ceremony had sanctified the union. The evangelist's long and outstanding service had placed him in such a conspicuous position in the little church in Canton, and indeed in the eyes of the Christian world, that any lapse on his part would have been a terrific blow. Having heard some talk about the matter a Baptist missionary asked Dr. Hobson whether he had complete confidence in Liang A-fa. He said the question was not prompted by any doubt of his sincerity, but in his own Mission several of their most promising assistants had fallen into sin and were lost to the Cause, bringing shame upon the Gospel. Dr. Hobson, having made careful investigation into the whole matter, was able to reply that he had the fullest confidence in A-fa's Christian character. He went on to say that he did not think it right to judge A-fa or any Chinese converted to Christianity by the same standard that missionaries should apply to themselves.

A-fa's last available letter to the Society is dated July 15, 1852, and was translated by his son. In it he summarizes the evangelistic work of the previous few years, dwelling specially on his fellowship with Dr. Hobson in the hospital and chapel, the personal benefit he had received from a better understanding of the Bible, and the joy of harvest that had been given them. He concludes by saying that although he is still strong, with good hearing and sight, a strong voice and healthy body, the work of preaching is so great that helpers are needed, and he asks for the cooperation of Christians in England by prayer and gift. The last sentence is the benediction: "May the blessing of Almighty God, Father, Son and Spirit be with you, my dear brothers and sisters, for ever and ever." Thus ends the last epistle of the Chinese apostle Liang A-fa.

An English visitor to the hospital during 1854 described a service in an article written to one of the London papers. He writes: "The patients were mustering early in the chapel seats, which by the hour of eleven were well nigh filled, and the places appropriated to those connected with the hospital were occupied. At that hour the aged evangelist Liang A-fa walked to the preacher's seat. The order of conducting the service was similar to that of Congregational churches at home, but the aged man follows the custom of his country's sages and sits to teach. On this occasion he expounded closely and vigorously St. Paul's address to the Athenians."[2]

The sidelight on the old preacher's habit of sitting when delivering his address raises the question whether this was only begun in later years or was his usual posture. Our ignorance on this point reminds us again that there are many things regarding the evangelist's life and work which are lost to us. For example, not one of the sources consulted has mentioned that he ever smiled or laughed. We judge from what is said about his books and addresses that he had the gift of apt illustration, and was able, as most Chinese preachers are, to draw both smiles and scowls by his ridiculing of idolatry and superstition. But life seems always to have been too serious a thing for him to be taken lightly. Of course the same might almost be said of Robert Morrison. Wells Williams described the pioneer missionary as "having no sprightliness nor pleasantry, and not by nature calculated to win and interest the skeptical or the fastidious."[3] A-fa in one of his letters to the secretary of the London Missionary Society, translated into English by his son, criticizes the Society for sending out middle-aged missionaries. He says their tongues are too stiff for adjustment to the peculiarities of the spoken language, and they are in so great a hurry to write books that the Chinese find it difficult to understand what they have written. He suggests that missionaries should be sent out when seven or eight years of age, while their tongues are pliable, and they still have time enough to study the written language. Whether this proposal indicates a sense of humor or its lack we have not been able to decide, but those of us who have spent the greater part of life in China would go further and wish we had begun with the language from the cradle—at least Dr. Milne thought the years of Methuselah might allow a reasonable time for mastering it. Well for us that most of our Chinese friends are so tolerant and kindly in their judgment.

As A-fa realized that his strength was gradually failing, he became more and more earnest about the spiritual state of his near relatives, and especially of his son. He repeatedly told them he was going Home and admonished them to take heed to his words and receive the Gospel. They would then be ready to follow him. The son had been away in Nanking and Tientsin assisting the British and American Plenipotentiaries it the task of treaty revision. When he returned in the autumn of 1854 he found his father in poorer health. A-teh urged him to give up his preaching at the hospital, but the old man replied that forty years had passed since the light of the Gospel had dawned on his mind, and knowing there was no other way to life eternal he could not bear to see his fellow-countrymen still in the darkness of spiritual death. He was determined to give his last breath in preaching the Gospel to them.

So the brave warrior carried on till the end. On the Saturday evening before his death, as his custom was, he bathed in preparation for the keeping of the Sabbath. In his weak state of health he caught a chill. But this did not prevent his crossing the river to take the Sunday service at the mission hospital. He preached with great earnestness from the text "Be not afraid of them which kill the body, but are not able to kill the soul; but rather fear him which is able to destroy both soul and body in hell." On the Monday he was back again at the hospital to preach for the last time to the assembled patients. Returning home he went to bed, but insisted on rising to take evening prayers in his own chapel. This resulted in another chill, and on the Tuesday the son went to tell Dr. Hobson his father was unwell and would be unable to come to the hospital and preach the next day. The doctor gave him some medicine, and sent a message urging the evangelist not to leave the house until he was stronger. But the old man knew the end was at hand. The medicine did him good, and he used the short respite it gave him to have a farewell talk with his beloved son. He recalled his cherished desire, when placing his boy under the care and tuition of Dr. Bridgman, that he might be prepared for the work of translating the Scriptures and preaching the Gospel. Now it seemed these hopes had been disappointed. But the work his son was doing in helping to promote amicable relations between China and other countries was that of a peacemaker, on whom Christ had pronounced a blessing. What troubled A-fa most was that official employment, particularly with the Chinese Government, meant working on the Sabbath. He urged him to accept only positions in which he could keep that day holy. He also exhorted him to teach his family the Bible, and to pray often with them, expressing the hope that from among his grandchildren there might be one who would be a translator of the Scriptures and a preacher. Although he had no material wealth to bequeath to his son he had given him a knowledge of the Scriptures, more precious than any worldly possession. The earnest prayer of his whole life was that all his descendants, from generation to generation, should be Christian.

Only two hours before his death the old man felt well enough to take a little food and then slept. Waking he asked for a drink of tea. When he had drunk he handed the cup to his son, and lifting up his eyes to heaven his lips moved in prayer. He then looked round on the faces of each one in the group beside his bed, closed his eyes, and suddenly passed away without a word or moan. Thus, about three o'clock in the morning of Thursday April 12, 1855, Liang A-fa went to be with Christ which is very far better.

The son crossed the river to tell Dr. Hobson, and the doctor went back with him accompanied by Messrs. Beech and Cox, recently arrived members of the Wesleyan Mission, and three Chinese Christians. With the family and friends gathered round the bed on which the body lay, portions of Scripture were read from the resurrection chapter in St Paul's letter to the Corinthians, and prayers were offered in Chinese. Mr. Cox closed the service with an appropriate prayer in English. The features of the dead saint were very natural, and sweetly composed as if in sleep.

Among those in the room when the old pilgrim triumphantly crossed the river and entered the City was A-teh's daughter "Autumn Gold" then eight years of age. She and her grandfather were very fond of each other. About ten years ago she, now an old woman herself, related her memories of that event to a veteran—the late Dr. J. C. Thomson—who was always keenly interested in preserving the memory of A-fa. Her grandfather had held her hand while he told them the Heavenly Father was calling him Home. She had a strange story to tell of the old man seeing a vision of a golden sedan chair coming to carry him to the King's palace. So peaceful and even joyous was his face after death that his missionary friends could only praise God for His goodness. In her sorrow the little girl refused to eat, and was only persuaded to do so when told it was her grandfather's wish. In later years this girl was married into a pagan home, and for half a century lived in superstition and idolatry. But she could never escape the memory of that Christian deathbed, and sixty years afterwards she came to a Wesleyan church in Wuchow seeking membership. Not only did she herself become an earnest Christian, but she persuaded her nieces also to give their lives to Christ. Thus was one of the last prayers of God's servant answered.

Dr. Hobson, writing next day to report the matter to the Society in London, pays the following tribute to his colleague: "He has now been intimately associated with me for seven years, and I rejoice to state that throughout the whole of that time I have never known him absent from his post, except very occasionally from temporary indisposition, nor flinching to declare as far as he knew it, the whole counsel of God to his apathetic and godless countrymen............ His Christian course has not been without admixture of infirmity and imperfection, but he has kept steadfastly to the truth as he has learned it in the Bible, and to the day of his death, never turned his back upon it, nor was ashamed of it in the presence of his enemies or friends............ His place will not soon be filled, and it may be long before we see his like again. He kept up, while alive, an interesting link with our noble predecessors, the one who baptized him and the one who set him apart to the work of an evangelist. Now he is gone, and we have no one left in this wide field of that generation .... May it please the

Head of the Church to let us see the fruit of the labors of His servant, and to raise up in his place many other devoted laborers who shall go in and out boldly declaring the Gospel of Jesus Christ."

Dr. Hobson also writes that the coffin containing the body of Liang A-fa was to be placed in the garden beside his house, under a cover to shelter it from the weather, until it would be safe to convey it to the family graveyard some miles distant, where his father and wife were already buried. A few weeks later Dr. Hobson wrote again that the funeral had taken place, but it left the home so early in the morning that only a few relatives were able to attend. Contemporary history explains the reason for uncertainty and fear. During the previous year there had been a rising of the lawless Triad Society, the members of which allied themselves with the Taiping rebels in the occupation of the large city of Fatshan, and gained command of the river branches and the open country around Canton. They had, however, no strong leader to unify their operations, and thus failed in the attempt to occupy Canton. The garrison in the provincial capital was able to secure volunteer recruits through the fear that the supplies of food on which the city was dependent would be cut off. The rebels were gradually dispersed. In Canton itself many thousands of the insurgents and their sympathizers were seized and executed. A Canton correspondent writing to the Hong Kong paper of the very month in which the death and burial of Liang A-fa took place says "If the month of April was called the starving month' in Canton, that of May should be called 'the bloody month', for such a succession of executions has not been known within the present generation. On an average more than two hundred have been executed daily in Canton city during the last fortnight." Under these disturbed conditions it was no small risk to visit the lonely spot outside the city where the family graves were situated. A-teh would have been considered, because of his official connection, a valuable prize if they had fallen in with robbers, of whom there are always many at such a time.

Not only were the Taiping rebels in the neighborhood of the city, but relations were again becoming more and more strained between China and Britain. These things made the year of Liang A-fa's death specially trying for the little church in the Hospital of Merciful Love. But in spite of the loss of their pioneer leader, and uncertainty regarding the future, it proved a year of unprecedented ingathering. Some fifteen persons, the sincerity of whose profession had long been tested, were received into the church from which the pastor had been taken. A large crowd of interested people witnessed their baptism. Thus again was the Scripture fulfilled: "Except a grain of wheat fall into the ground and die it abideth by itself alone; but if it die it beareth much fruit."

Illustration 14.1: "Autumn Gold" in old age. Died some years ago in Kwangsi.

Illustration 14.2: A Christian great granddaughter of Liang A-fa
with her husband and children.

Notes

1. Samuel Augustus Tipple (born circa 1827) published books of sermons in the 1870s through the 1890s.

2. According to Gerald H. Choa, *'Heal the Sick' Was Their Motto: The Protestant Medical Missionaries in China* (Hong Kong: The Chinese University of Hong Kong, 1990), 55, this quote is from "a London journal in 1854 and reproduced by [William] Lockhart" (1811–1896), the first British medical missionary to China.

3. Marshall Broomhall, *Robert Morrison: A Master Builder* (London: Student Christian Movement, 1927), 225.

15

After Many Days

"The Church itself............... The work of no ordinary builders! Sometimes the work goes forward in deep darkness: sometimes in blinding light: now beneath the burden of unutterable anguish; now to the tune of a great laughter and heroic shoutings like the cry of thunder. Sometimes, in the silence of the night time, one may hear the tiny hammerings of the comrades at work up in the dome—the comrades that have climbed ahead."[1]

—MANSON

Francis Bacon said, "It is the true office of history to represent the events themselves, and to leave the observations and conclusions thereupon to the liberty and faculty of every man's judgment." But the biography of a man like Liang A-fa, specially one written so long afterwards, cannot be complete if it rings down the curtain on the funeral. Readers naturally wish to know what influence his life has had during the intervening years.

The Rev. George Smith wrote in 1844 of Liang A-teh, the evangelist's son: "He is a smart, intelligent, and well-educated young man. The high pay which he receives (as English translator in a leading Chinese firm) places him far above the rank of his father, and though the influence for good of such an individual in the Government offices may be extensive in improving the tone of international intercourse, yet it is difficult to banish regret from the mind that for direct Christian missionary work he is practically lost to us. The case of A-teh appears to be a specimen of the difficulty and disappointment to which our missions will for some years be necessarily exposed, unless the English language be excluded from mission schools."[2] The last sentence raises a controversial issue over which many doughty champions of rival theories have broken lances. The case of Hoh Tsun-shin—Dr. Legge's assistant and the first pastor of a Chinese church in Hong Kong—would seem to prove the contrary. The fact remains that A-teh was never vitally interested in Christian work. In response to the urgent pleading of his father he occasionally gave a little help in teaching or translation, but after the father's death he had no further direct connection with the church. That several of his missionary friends left their regular work to represent their Governments in official positions may have salved his conscience to a certain extent. Dr. Hobson says that in spite of his father's prayers and tears and solemn pleadings on his deathbed, the son gave no evidence of genuine Christian faith, and had ceased to join in public worship. His only son's refusal to let Christ control the life on which such high hopes had been set, was the heaviest cross Liang A-fa carried.

When the Chinese Maritime Customs was organized A-teh found employment under Mr. H. N. Lay in opening up new stations in various provinces. Subsequently he was assigned to Chaochow, where he acted as head clerk and deputy commissioner for five years. When Mr. Lay resigned and Mr. (afterwards Sir) Robert Hart took office A-teh continued in the service until he was forty-two years of age. He then left on account of ill health and returned to Canton, where he died at his ancestral village in middle life. His grave is marked by a simple granite slab on a hillock beside the flood-dyke path just outside the village of Lohtsun.

He had eight children, two of whom died in infancy. Of the sons one went to a northern province, and no news of what happened to him came back to his relatives. One after another the brothers died, leaving no male issue. Finally only one was left, the fifth son, named Chaak Laan (Watered Magnolia) who lived in his grandfather's house on Honam. He had a number of daughters and one boy—Taat Ming (Illustrious). Liang Chaak Laan was a member of the gentry in his community, a position which gave him standing as a justice of the peace. He claimed to be an ardent Confucianist, and would have nothing to do with Christianity. It seemed as if the grandfather's influence within his own family was lost, and his prayers unanswered. Then A-teh's daughter—Autumn Gold—returned in her old age to the faith of early childhood. She came to her brother's home on Honam—the home of her deepest impressions—and persuaded three nieces to visit her at Wuchow. There they attended a Christian school and came back to Canton to live changed lives. But the old father withstood their prayers and pleadings. He fell ill and the daughters were more insistent that he should receive God's love into his heart. At last he consented to their inviting the preacher of the church which they attended to come and visit him. When Mr. Lee sat beside his bed the sick man opened his heart to him. He said he knew the end was near and hungered for a sure hope on which to lean. He now believed Jesus was the Divine Savior and was ready to trust in Him alone. Thus, at the age of sixty-three, in the evening of his days, Liang A-fa's last grandson was baptized in the home where the evangelist had so often preached the Gospel, and from which he had been translated. His body was laid in that historic God's acre—the Protestant cemetery beside the road leading from the city to the White Cloud Hills. Taat Ming was a fine boy and had joined his sisters in accepting Christ. They were desirous he should enter the Christian College, be trained as a preacher, and follow in the footsteps of his great-grandfather. But at fourteen years of age he too was called away, leaving the family of Liang A-fa without male descendant.

Fifty years after Pastor Liang's death the Canton Christian College (Lingnan University) moved from temporary quarters at Macao to a site near Honglok Village on Honam Island. As the college developed, more and more land had to be secured for the campus. For generations the higher land in the neighborhood had been used as a burial ground. Many graves had to be purchased and the owners compensated so that the bones might be removed and interred elsewhere. During the course of such negotiations the then Chinese vice-president of the College—Mr. W. K. Chung—received a letter from a Mr. Fung of Kuala Lumpur in the Malay States saying his wife was a great-granddaughter of the first Protestant evangelist in China, and that this pioneer preacher's grave was included in land which the institution was purchasing for further extension. Mr. Fung was a catechist connected with the Methodist Church. Careful investigation proved that his statement was undoubtedly true.

In the Summer of 1918 the annual conference of preachers from different parts of the Kwangtung province gathered at the Christian College. Mr. Chung conducted them to Liang A-fa's grave on Phoenix Hill, and as they stood around that hallowed spot—the first Christian group since the burial so long before—the present generation of evangelists was brought into touch with their noble predecessor, who had been almost completely forgotten. When the graves in that area were removed the remains of Liang A-fa were reinterred at the centre of the college campus, on the site reserved for the college chapel. This now sacred plot was dedicated on Founder's

Day—June 7, 1922. The second General Assembly of the Church of Christ in China met at Canton in 1930 and the delegates went on pilgrimage to the grave. The Moderator—Dr. C. Y. Cheng—conducted a memorial service and planted an *arbor vitae* (a tree of life).

Resulting from the revived interest following the publication of the biography in Chinese, investigations have been begun in Liang A-fa's district of Koming which reveal the fact that it been sadly neglected by the church. While neighboring districts have many churches with a strong membership this had only one small chapel with less than twenty members, and this amidst an estimated population of one hundred thousand people. What could speak more pathetically of the degree to which the first evangelist has been forgotten, or plead more loudly that the earliest efforts of over a century ago should be renewed. During this year (1933) the village of Lohtsun has been visited by representatives of the church. The old house rebuilt by Liang A-fa after the flood of 1833 is still standing, but is fast falling into decay. When visited last the building was being used as a dump for the refuse of the mulberry leaves after the edible parts had been devoured by silkworms. That waste heap on the dirty floor of the dilapidated dwelling suggests a parable. It represents part of the process which gives the world its most costly and beautiful silk. It reminds us the apostles were made "as the refuse of the world, the offscouring of all things." As one stood amidst these crumbling beams and tottering walls the mind went back over the life story outlined in these pages, and the forsaken ruins and rubbish heaps were forgotten in the sense that one was standing on holy ground. But to his fellow-villagers that hovel speaks of the deserved desolation of the man who forsook the faith of his fathers, and drew the wrath of Heaven upon himself and the anger of the officials on his innocent clansmen.

Apart from occasional visits and the cultivation of friendly contacts little direct Christian work can be done in this village while the first prophet has so little honor in his own country and among his own people. A mile away on the further side of the river, however, the long market town of Samchow bestraddles the broad flood dyke. There, where the lad A-fa was sent on market days to purchase the family supplies, the church has found its opportunity. Inexpensive buildings have been rented in which a preacher is stationed with his family. A few scattered Christians from the market and outlying villages have been gathered for Sunday services. Some of these had almost forgotten what public worship was like. Their witness had long ago ceased to be effective. One had been a preacher, but the opium habit had drugged him into spiritual stupor. He is now the most active voluntary worker and the enemy is under his feet. Meetings held several evenings a week are attended by audiences that overflow from the small hall right across the quiet side street. A matting roof has been erected to shelter from sun and rain. A reading room draws a constant and steadily increasing group of those who have caught a glimpse of a wider world and wish to learn more. The use of a few standard remedies and a little knowledge of nursing bring sick folk seeking help. The preacher is trying to assist the farmers around with some of their difficult agricultural problems. When he is up against things too hard for him he comes to some of the experts in the city and enlists their cooperation. The work has only begun, but already he, with his wife and friends, are making the Liang A-fa Memorial Centre a minister of that more abundant life which Jesus came to bring.

Preacher Lei is sometimes taunted with the fact that Liang A-fa's old home seems to have no owner and he has none left to light the lamp before the ancestral shrine. He replies that the pioneer evangelist's spiritual children are without number, and that the warmth and light and power of the flame he kindled are spreading throughout the whole of China and influencing every part of her new life.

But, as Dr. Sun stated in his will, "the revolution is not yet complete."[3] It is only beginning. The poverty, ignorance, superstition and sin of Liang A-fa's own village and district, along with myriads like it, and the hopeless failure to secure for the Republic of China that integrity, intelligence, unity, and independence without which it cannot progress to an honored place among the nations, are a trumpet call to the Church, The history of the past century (and all the centuries *anno domini*) have proved that Jesus Christ is the one Savior of men. The Chinese Church is not deaf to the bugle call for advance. She is ready for her rightful place in the van. She feels though, and is saying so most insistently and pleadingly, that the time has not yet come when the Church in the West can lay down the responsibility it first accepted in the partnership between Robert Morrison and Liang A-fa.

Notes

1. This is a line of dialogue from Charles Rann Kennedy's play *The Servant in the House*, which was performed in 1906 and published in 1908.

2. George Smith, *A Narrative of an Exploratory Visit to Each of the Consular Cities of China* (New York: Harper & Brothers, 1857), 45–46.

3. Sun Yat-sen (1866–1925) is often called the father of modern China. His revolution was claimed by the two parties that competed for China following his death, the Communists and the Nationalists (or Guomindang).

Glossary

Character	Pinyin	English/ Old Romanization
按手	anshou	ordain
澳門	Aomen	Macao
拜上帝會	Bai Shangdi Hui	Society of God; God worshipping society
寶卷	baojuan	precious volumes
博愛者	Bo'aizhe	"Catholic Lover" (Milne's penname)
佈道者	budaozhe	preacher; evangelist
蔡亞高	Cai Agao	Tsae A-ko
東印度公司	Dong Yindu Gongsi	East India Company
惡根	egen	evil source, evil root
福音	fuyin	gospel
高明縣	Gaoming xian	Koming (district)
廣東	Guangdong	Kwangtung
廣州	Guangzhou	Canton
觀音	Guanyin	Kwanyin
古勞村	Gulao cun	Lohtsun (village)
河南	Henan	Honom (city)
何進善	He Jinshan	Ho Tsun Shin
洪秀全	Hong Xiuquan	Hung Siu-tsuen
惠愛醫院	Hui'ai Yiyuan	Hospital of Merciful Love
江門	Jiangmen	Kongmoon
基督教	Jidujiao	Protestantism
極樂世界	Jileshijie	the Sukhavati World
景教	Jingjiao	Church of the East ("Nestorianism")
經文	jingwen	text, tract
救世	jiushi	salvation, save the world

Glossary

救世主	Jiushizhu	Lord who Saves the World; Savior
救世主耶穌	Jiushizhu Yesu	Jesus, Savior of the World
卷	juan	volume, chapter
孔教	Kongjiao	Confucianism
魁星	Kuixing	God of literature
賴	Lai	Lai (a surname)
老師	laoshi	teacher
梁發	Liang Fa	Liang Fa
梁進德	Liang Jinde	Leang Tsen-teh
良言	liang yan	good words
兩友相論	*Liangyou xianglun*	*Conversation Between Two Friends* (a tract)
伶仃島	Lingding Dao	Lintin Island
嶺南大學	Lingnan Daxue	Lingnan University
理雅各	Liyage	(James) Legge
亂	luan	disordered, chaotic
倫敦會	Lundun Hui	London (Missionary) Society
馬禮遜	Malixun	(Robert) Morrison
麻六甲	Maliujia	Malacca (Malaya)
滿洲	Manzhou	Manchu, Manchuria
米憐	Milian	(Wiliam) Milne
牧師	mushi	pastor, shepherd
牧者	muzhe	pastor, shepherd
南海縣	Nanhai xian	Nanhai district
乾隆	Qianlong	(The Emperor) Kien Lung
秋金	Qiu Jin	Autumn Gold
勸	quan	admonish, exhort
勸世良言	*Quanshi liangyan*	*Good News to Admonish the World*
勸世文	quanshiwen	tract
日記言行	*Riji yanxing*	*Diary of Words and Deeds*
儒釋道	ru shi dao	Confucianism, Buddhism, Daoism
三教	sanjiao	three teachings, three religions
三洲	Sanzhou	Samchow
三字經	*Sanzijing*	*Three Character Classic*

上帝	Shangdi	"ruler on high," God
善書	shanshu	good book, morality book
蛇魔	shemo	snake demon (the devil)
神	shen	god, divinity
神天上帝	shentian shangdi	God, the Heavenly Lord on High
神爺火華	Shen Yehuohua	God Jehovah, Fiery Father God of China
神風	Shenfeng	Holy Spirit (old term)
神聖風	Shen Shengfeng	God the Holy Spirit
聖靈	Shengling	Holy Spirit (newer term)
世	shi	world, generation
十戒	shi jie	Ten Commandments
十三行	Shisan heng	Shih-san Hong, the thirteen hong merchants
四書五經	Sishu Wujing	Four Books, Five Classics
孫中山	Sun Zhongshan	Sun Yatsen
太平天國	Taiping Tianguo	Taiping Heavenly Kingdom
泰山	Taishan	Mt. Tai
天	tian	heaven
天地之大主	Tiandi zhi dazhu	Great Lord of Heaven and Earth
天主教	Tianzhujiao	Catholicism
文昌	Wenchang	God of literature
黃埔	Huangpu	Whampoa
西安	Xi'an	Xian
香港	Xianggang	Hong Kong
先生	xiansheng	"teacher"
行惡	xinge	follow wickedness
行善	xingshan	follow goodness
學善者	Xueshanzhe	"the one who studies goodness" (penname)
新加坡	Xinjiapo	Singapore
鴉片	yapian	opium
英華字典	*Yinghua Zidian*	Anglo-Chinese Dictionary
英華書店	Yinghua Shudian	Anglo-Chinese College
中國	Zhongguo	China

Index

Abeel, Rev. D., impressions of Liang A-fa, 51–52

A-gong, conversion, work and discipleship, 51–53, 82–84, 93, 99–100

Ainsworth, Percy, quoted, 7

Anglo-Chinese College
founded at Malacca, 29–30
transferred to Hong Kong, 92–93

A-teh, Liang A-fa's son
assisting British and American plenipotentiaries, 109
baptized, 41
born, 35
Commissioner Lin's English translator, xxx, 86
death, 116
education, 66–67
Engaged by Powtinqua, merchant, 93
lost to Missions, 115
used by Commissioner Ke-ying, 93–94

"Autumn Gold," A-fa's granddaughter, 111, 113

Banyan trees, 8, 15

Buddhism, xxvi–xxvii
a Buddhist Abbot, 96
Boldness of A-fa, 67–71, 112

Britain and China—first war, 92–96

British trade relations, 18

Burns, Rev. W. C., quoted, 99

Biographical records, difficulty in securing, x, 3–4

Call to the Church today, 119

Canton Hospital, 100–101

Chau, Pastor, conversion and work, 105–6

Chinese abroad, 31

Chinese religious inheritance, 40

Christian Home influence of, 34

Church History
value of study, 1
difficulty in getting data, 3, 4

Church Missionary Society, deputation, 96

Converts, criticism of
refuted, 20

Cooperation
Church and Missions, 3
Medical and evangelistic work, 105

Descendants of Liang A-fa, 115–17

Devolution, 2

Difficulties of Christian converts, 20, 33–34

Dyer, Rev. S., 83–84

East and West, beginning of struggle, 85–86

East India Company and Morrison, 18

Education,
of Chinese boys, 10–11
and Christianity, 48–49
in English, criticism of, 115

Examination Hall, 53, 68

Evangelism, xxv
  conversational, 60–65
  and education, 48
  Liang A-fa's urge, xxiv, 58
  a liberal interpretation, 84
  through literature, 68, 75, 79,
    105–6
  and medical work, 83, 102–6

Faithfulness of A-fa, xxiv, 104
First Chinese Protestant Christian to
    win his wife for Christ, 35–36
First Chinese Protestant Christian to
    present his child for baptism,
    40
First Chinese Protestant Christian to
    suffer beating, imprisonment,
    and banishment for Christ's
    sake, xxii–xxiii, 33–34, 70–71,
    84
First Chinese Protestant Christian to
    write a tract, 33
First Chinese Protestant evangelist,
    xxv, 41–42
First evangelist to carry the Gospel
    into the interior, 51
First hospital evangelist in China,
    100–103
First to open a Protestant school in
    China, 49
First pastor of a regular Protestant
    congregation in China, 103
First Protestant convert [Tsae A-ko],
    21–22
First to receive a Chinese woman
    into the Protestant Church,
    35–36
First to use literature in reaching the
    literati in China, 53, 66
Foreign factories, 12, 20, 38
Foreign missionaries, functions of, 3
Foreign Powers and China,
    beginning of struggle, 88
    treaties, 91, 95–96

Gairdner of Cairo, quoted, 47
Gillespie, Rev. W., 22, 100
Grave of Liang A-fa, xli, 5, 90, 112,
    118

Hart, Sir Robert, quoted, 18
Ho Tsun Shin, education, eloquence,
    and faithfulness, 93, 116
Hobson, Dr. B., 5, 66, 86, 88,
    102–12, 116
Home life of A-fa, 56–60
Hong Kong ceded, 92
Hospital work, xxv, 83, 87, 95,
    100–112
Hung Jin ("Shield King"), 77
Hung Siu-tsuen and Taiping Rebel-
    lion, 75–79

Kew A-gong, conversion, disciple-
    ship, and work, 50–53, 93,
    99–100
Ke-ying, Commissioner and
    Viceroy, 93–95
Kochow, work among literati, 53, 60
Koming District, 7, 51, 118
Kwu, Teacher, A-fa's first convert,
    48–49, 56

Lam, the innkeeper, 60–65
Lamqua, artist, 102, 106
Lay, G. T., 83
Legge, Dr. J., ix, 22, 77, 93, 99–100,
    116
Letters of Liang A-fa to L.M.S., xii,
    xxii, 4, 11, 44, 46, 48, 54, 67,
    95, 108–9
Lew Tse Chuen, the fruit of
    Christian literature and per-
    sonal work, 81
LIANG A-FA
  in Anglo-Chinese College,
    Malacca, 86–87
  arrest, escape, flight, 70
  back to Canton, 35

LIANG A-FA (*cont.*)
banished from Canton, 34
baptism, xviii, xx–xxii, 25–30
biographical data, x, 3–4
birth and birthplace, 7–8
boldness, 67, 69
builds house and preaching hall
on Honam, 102
conversion, xiv–xxii, 25–29
death and burial, 110–111
declining health, 109
early education, 10
early religious impressions,
11–12, 20
effort to avert war, 85
estrangement from A–gong and
reconciliation, 99
evangelistic work in Canton, 85
family poverty, 11–12
first contact with Morrison and
the Gospel, 20
first fruits of personal work [bap-
tism of Kwu], 48
first letter to L.M.S., 44–45
first missionary journey, 52–53
fruitful years, 66
further studies at Macao, 47–48
grave at Lingnan campus, 117
his father, 40, 47, 67, 93
in his home, 57–58
his mother, 11
hospital evangelist, 100–103
issues first tract, 33
last letter to L.M.S., 108
learning printing, 13
letter to L.M.S., 48–49
Liang A-fa memorial centre, 119
leaving home, 12
to Malacca, 34
to Malacca to study for ministry,
36
to Malacca with Milne, 21
marriage, 32–33
Morrison's commendation, 42

name, 9–10
natural temper, 47
opens a school, 49
ordained, 41–42
passing on the torch, 105
persecution, xxii, 33–34
personal work, 60–64
question ordination, 42
re-marriage, 107
residence in Honam, 87, 89
return to Canton, 20, 40, 84
seeking the Truth, 24
to Singapore and Malacca, 71, 82
son, born, 35
strong in prayer, 47
studies and tract writing in Canton, 49–50
studying the Scriptures, 24–25
testimony of Rev. George Smith,
96
welcomes Bridgman and Abeel,
51
wife, 35–36
Lin, Commissioner, 84–88
Literati, work among, 45, 53, 66, 75
Literature
effect on rebel leader, 77
fruits of, 81–82
Lohtsun village, 7–8, 12, 14, 35,
52, 55, 87, 116, 118
needs to be supplemented by
personal contact, 79
London Missionary Society, ix
headquarters at Malacca, 21
relics of Liang A–fa, 4
transferred to Hong Kong, 92

Macao, 18, 21–23, 29, 35, 41–42, 47,
49–50, 69–71, 83–84, 86–88,
95, 105, 117
Mackintosh, Prof. H. R., quoted, 24
Malacca, L.M.S. Mission centre, 21,
83–84, 92
Manson, quoted, 115

McNeur, George H., xi–xiii
Meadows, T. T., tribute to Liang
    A-fa, 78
Medhurst, Dr., xii, xiv, xx, xxv, 77,
    80–83, 88
Medical Mission work, 87, 99–103
Memorial centre to Liang A-fa, 119
Milne, Dr. W., xii, xiv–xv, xx–xiv, 5
    appreciation of work, 36
    arrival in China, 21
    death, 36
    influence on Liang A-fa, 21, 26
    first principal Anglo-Chinese
        College, Malacca, 29–30
    Glasgow University confers D.D.,
        34
    stationed in Malacca, 21
Milne, Mrs. W.
    death, 31
    influence on Liang A-fa, 31
Milne, Rev. W. C. (son of Dr. W.
    Milne)
    arrival in China, 86
    and Liang A-fa, 86–87
Morrison, Dr. Robert, ix
    baptizes first Protestant convert,
        22–23
    centenary of death, 2, bicenten-
        nial, xiv
    early prayer, 14
    failing health, 68
    first days in Canton, 18
    furlough, 41–42
    Glasgow University confers D.D.,
        34
    joined by Bridgman, 51
    last service and death, 69
    ordains Liang A-fa, xxiii–xxv,
        35, 42
    the pioneer, 18
    plans for Anglo-Chinese College
        materialize, 29
    return to China, 42
    temperament, 57

testimony to Liang A-fa, 44,
    47–48
translating Scriptures, 19
Morrison, John R. (eldest son of Dr.
    Morrison)
    Chinese translator to British
        merchants in Canton, 68
    death, 94
    help in trouble, 70–71, 85
    "Most favored nation" clause, 95
Mott, John R., quoted, xii, 1

Names, giving of, in China, xx, 9–10
Nanking, Treaty of, 92
Napier, Lord, 69, 71, 84

Objections to Christianity answered
    by A-fa, 49–50
Opium, xxix, xxx, 84–85, 91, 118

Parker, Dr. Peter, viii, 5, 73, 83, 97,
    100, 106
Persecution, xxiii, 2, 20, 33, 44, 67,
    71, 82, 84
Personal evangelism, vii, xv, 48–49,
    57, 59–63, 65, 81–82
Prayer, xx, xxxii, xxxvi, xliii
    answered, 111
    first Sino-American–British
        meeting for, 51
    Ke-ying's, 94
    Liang A-fa's strong point, 47
    Printing from wooden blocks, 13
Printing Scriptures forbidden, 19

Religious inheritance of China, 40,
    43
Roberts, Rev. I. J., and Tai-ping
    Rebellion, 76–77
Rutherford, Samuel, quoted, 31, 39

Samchow market town, 7–8, 12, 58,
    70, 89–90, 118
Scripture lessons, 67–68

Scripture translation, xviii, xxviii,
xxxiv, xxxvii, 19, 24, 26, 67, 78
"Shield King," Hung Jin, 77
Sino-American-British first missionary prayer meeting, 51
Smith, Rev. George
first Bishop of Victoria, Hong
Kong, 5, 96
and Liang A-fa, 5, 96–98
quoted, 5, 115
seeking quarters in Canton, 96
Social welfare work, 84
Spiritual heritage of Chinese Christians, 2

Taiping Rebellion, ix, xiii, xiv–xviii,
xxix, xxxii, xxxiv, xxxvii, 75,
77–78, 80, 112, 123
Thomson, Dr. J. C., 111
Three Character Classic, 10
Tipple, S. A., quoted, 107
Toleration, 95
Tracts
composed and printed by Liang
A-fa, 29, 50–52
"The Conversation between Two
Friends," 36, 105
distribution, 50–52, 61, 75–76,
105
efficacy of, testimony by T. T.
Meadows, 78

relation to Taiping rebellion, xiii,
xviii, 75, 78
Translation of the Scriptures,
xxviii, xxxiv, xxxvii, 19, 24,
26, 36, 67, 78, 110
Treaties with Foreign Powers,
95–96, 101
Treaty ports, 92, 96, 100
Tsae A-ko, first Protestant convert,
xxi, 22–23, 33

"Unequal Treaties," 95

Vaccination for small-pox, 40

War between Britain and China,
85, 92
Wells Williams, xii, 21, 67, 77, 80,
109
impressions of Liang A-fa, 67
on Taiping movement, 77

Yui, Dr. David Z. T., quoted, xiii, 92

*This index is edited and repaginated
from the original.*

www.ingramcontent.com/pod-product-compliance
Lightning Source LLC
Chambersburg PA
CBHW060342100426
42812CB00003B/1088